To Jean,
Welcome to my w..

Larry
6-11-13

Extraordinary inspirational
stories from the heart of the
Middle East conflict

VOICES FROM
ARMAGEDDON

LARRY RICH

ACKNOWLEDGEMENTS

I would like to express my love and
gratitude to the following people:

Carole Gotlieb, my former partner, for
encouraging me to write the stories that
I shared with her regularly and to seek
their publication. Carole, a talented
writer, had the courage and literary
wisdom to challenge me when necessary
and was influential in keeping my
writing focused.

Jeffrey Rich, my brother, for believing in
the power of these stories to alter
people's perceptions.

Jane Berman, a dear friend and fellow
writer who never doubted my ability to
tell these stories and stirred me to do so.

John Hunt, my publisher, for believing
in *Voices* and supporting me through the
final manuscript.

DEDICATION

*This book is dedicated to the
men, women and children of the
Valley of Armageddon who live
the reality of coexistence.*

Copyright © 2005 O Books
O Books is an imprint of John Hunt Publishing Ltd., The Bothy,
Deershot Lodge, Park Lane, Ropley, Hants, SO24 0BE, UK
office@johnhunt-publishing.com
www.O-books.net

Distribution in:
UK
Orca Book Services
orders@orcabookservices.co.uk
Tel: 01202 665432 Fax: 01202 666219 Int. code (44)

USA and Canada
NBN
custserv@nbnbooks.com
Tel: 1 800 462 6420 Fax: 1 800 338 4550

Australia
Brumby Books
sales@brumbybooks.com
Tel: 61 3 9761 5535 Fax: 61 3 9761 7095

New Zealand
Peaceful Living
books@peaceful-living.co.nz
Tel: 64 7 57 18105 Fax: 64 7 57 18513

Singapore
STP
davidbuckland@tlp.com.sg
Tel: 65 6276 Fax: 65 6276 7119

South Africa
Alternative Books
altbook@global.co.za
Tel: 27 011 792 7730 Fax: 27 011 972 7787

Text: © Larry Rich 2005

Design; Text and Cover: BookDesign™, London

ISBN 1 905047 56 8

A CIP catalogue record for this book is available from the
British Library. Printed in the USA by Maple-Vail
Manufacturing Group

EXTRAORDINARY INSPIRATIONAL
STORIES FROM THE HEART OF THE
MIDDLE EAST CONFLICT

VOICES FROM
ARMAGEDDON

LARRY RICH

BOOKS

WINCHESTER UK
NEW YORK USA

CONTENTS

INTRODUCTION

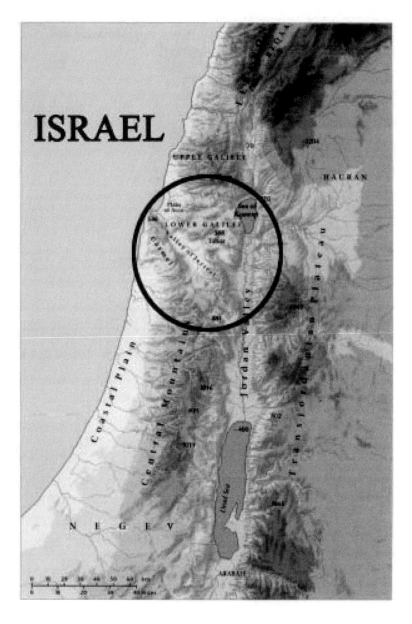

Figure 1 The Valley of Armgeddon

"The world is not respectable; it is mortal, tormented, confused, deluded forever; but it is shot through with beauty, with love, with glints of courage and laughter; and in these, the spirit blooms timidly, and struggles to the light amid the thorns."

George Santayana

When you hear the name Armageddon you probably conjure up images rooted in myth or the Bible. Armageddon is synonymous with The Apocalypse – Judgment Day – The End of Times. Students of the Bible know it as the place where the cataclysmic battle between the forces of good and evil will unfold and many believe that this battle will take place in the very near future. But it is also a real place, inhabited today by tens of thousands of people. In addition, it has already seen more fighting and bloodshed than any other spot on earth.

"Armageddon" comes from the Hebrew *Har Megiddo* and means literally "the mount of Megiddo." Tel (hill) Megiddo is a fascinating site where twenty cities have been built directly on top of one another and it lies at a strategic junction of roads running north–south and east–west (figure 3). Whoever had control of Mediddo had control of one of the major trade routes of antiquity, the Via Maris or, the "Way of the Sea" (figures 3, 4 and 5).

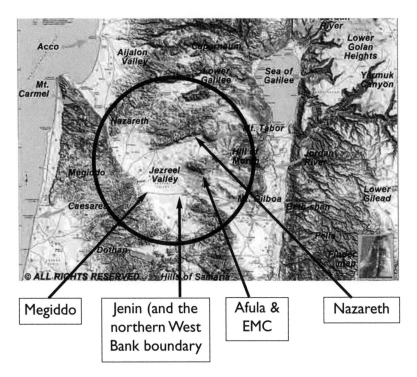

| Megiddo | Jenin (and the northern West Bank boundary | Afula & EMC | Nazareth |

Figure 2 Megiddo, Nazareth, Afula and EMC, Jenin

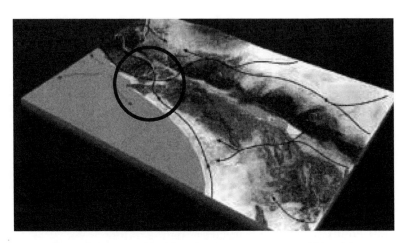

Figure 3 Historic Via Maris land route junction of Megiddo

Virtually every invading army that came through this region during the past 4000 years fought battles to dominate it and at least thirty-four bloody conflicts have already been fought at the ancient site of Megiddo and adjacent areas within the Jezreel Valley (see figures 1 and 2). Egyptians, Canaanites, Israelites, Midianites, Amalekites, Philistines, Hasmonaeans, Greeks, Romans, Muslims, Crusaders, Mamlukes, Mongols, French, Ottomans, British, Australians, Germans, Muslims and Israelis have all fought and died here. The names of the warring generals and leaders reverberate throughout history: Thutmose III, Deborah and Barak, Sisera, Gideon, Saul and Jonathan, Shishak, Jehu, Joram, Jezebel, Josiah, Antiochus, Ptolemy, Vespasian, Saladin, Napoleon, and Allenby, to name some of the most famous.

History seems to be teaching us the importance of maintaining a strategic presence on military and/or mercantile routes.

Megiddo and the Jezreel Valley have been Ground Zero for battles that determined the very course of civilization. It is no wonder that John, the author of Revelation, believed that the ultimate battle between good and evil would also take place in this region. He may yet prove to be right, as the conflict around the Valley is at the center of one of the world's most explosive disputes; one that could erupt into a nuclear Armageddon.

It follows that people who live in this region have unwittingly placed themselves in harm's way. The combination of historical facts, current realities and prophecy seems to have doomed the local inhabitants of Megiddo and the Jezreel Valley to a fate of unavoidable hate and bloodshed.

Who are these people and where do they live today? They are the Jews and Muslims of Israel living in Afula, Nazareth (figure 2), Beit She'an and tens of other villages, *kibbutzim* (cooperative farming settlements) and municipalities. Sharing the land and separated by a once invisible line that now boasts an electronic fence, impassable ditches and Israeli military patrols are the Muslims of the Palestinian Authority. They live along the southern fringe of the Jezreel Valley, known today as the Northern West Bank. This area's best-known town, Jenin (figure 2), is surrounded by tens of smaller Muslim villages.

The primary religions of those residing in the Jezreel Valley include Jews, Muslims, Christians and Druze. (The Druze are Arab descendants of Jethro, the father-in-law of Moses. They practice a secret religion that does not conform to traditional Islam.) Other than a handful who can trace their ancestry back several centuries, these neighbors (Muslims and Jews) have all immigrated from Egypt, Algeria, Morocco, Syria, Tunisia, Iraq, Iran, Ethiopia, Russia, Europe, the United States, South

America, South Africa, Canada, Saudi Arabia, Yemen, Jordan, Lebanon, Libya, the Philippines, Mexico and the Far East – to name just a few of their countries of origin. Today they all fall into one of two modern population categories, either Israeli or Palestinian. And here they live side by side in the Jezreel Valley. Megiddo. Armageddon.

Are these people destined to carry on an unwritten tradition of hatred and bloodshed? Are they inextricably caught in a vortex of historical violence? Have the crossroads of Via Maris sealed their fate? Do they have any say in their own futures or that of their children and grandchildren? And what about the fate of *your* families … if the conflict is not resolved?

The newspapers of the world reflect the stories that would have us believe the worst. The Muslims and Jews of Armageddon have inflicted upon one another unimaginable suffering and the fear that drives them seems to be the dominant force of the region.

However, there is another reality … a quiet, almost unspoken alternative truth. One place where this can be witnessed by anyone who cares to focus on a phenomenon that defies popular conception is in an exceptional medical institution.

Facing East/Southeast from Tel Megiddo today

Figure 4

Modern road today following the route of Via Maris

Figure 5

Figure 4 and 5 Modern road today, following the route of Via Maris

There is a community hospital standing in Afula at the gateway to the Jezreel Valley (figures 2 and 5) and it is called the *Emek* (Hebrew for Valley) *Medical Center* (EMC). The unique region it serves is equally divided between Jews and Muslims, its patient base reflecting this demographic reality. The staff is a multi-ethnic mix of Jews, Muslims, Christians and Druze. EMC is the only hospital in the Valley of Armageddon and, as a result of the violence and ongoing conflict in the region, has treated a very high number of horrific casualties.

Since October 2000, this hospital alone in a sparsely populated region has treated more than 800 victims of senseless and savage terror. Had the same level of terror taken place in New York, this would be the statistical equivalent of 150,000 wounded!

On an hourly basis, anyone can witness Jews saving Muslims and Christians, Muslims saving Jews and Christians while Christians are saving Muslims and Jews. The historical imprint of hate seems to vanish at the entrance to EMC – an isolated island of sanity in a region gone mad.

Living on the northwest fringe of the Jezreel Valley, I have been professionally involved with EMC since 1997. I am witness to the human dramas taking place daily between the Jews, Muslims, Christians and Druze of Israel. Muslims from Jenin (labeled the Palestinian capital of terror because many of the suicide bombers originated from there) arrive on EMC's doorstep seeking medical treatment. Nobody has ever been turned away.

The following pages will reveal true stories of everyday people living in the Valley of Armageddon, how they have been victimized by the conflict and yet managed to maintain their humanity.

These people are a living testament to the reality of hope. They show how human dignity and mutual respect take precedence over the blind hatred of those who would plunge this region and the world into a final holocaust.

These voices from Armageddon are echoes not normally heard from this historically damned region.

Author's note

Although the following stories are all true, many of the actual names have been altered or omitted. This is to protect those individuals from being wrongfully ostracized by their own people.

A VIPER, SALAAM AND HOPE

"I have been a stranger in a strange land." *Exodus 2:22*

They live in Palestinian Jenin. Thirteen-year-old Salaam (Arabic for peace), her mother Kamla, her father Basam, two older brothers and a younger sister. When Salaam was born in 1991, her family had already begun to feel the economic pressures resulting from the souring relations between their community and the neighboring Israelis. In a gesture of hope and devout belief in Allah (God), Basam and Kamla named their third child Salaam. They yearned for a productive and tranquil life and were confident that in calling their daughter "Peace" they would in some way influence the negative forces surrounding them.

Basam worked as an automobile mechanic in a local Jenin garage. Throughout the 1990s the modest enterprise enjoyed the business of neighboring Israelis who preferred the unpretentious services of the talented Arabs to their own state-of-the-art repair centers. He earned an honest living in a less than perfect existence, yet he provided for his family with dignity.

That all changed in October 2000. Anger and frustration among his people fueled by religious and political extremists erupted in an orgy of hate, killing and destruction. The second (Al Aqsa) *intifada* (uprising) had begun. The armed and well-organized fanatics among his people regarded every Israeli as a legitimate target and the neighboring city of Afula as worthy of destruction.

Young men and women were indoctrinated, brainwashed, "blessed" and dispatched into the Jezreel Valley with explosives strapped to their bodies. Their targets were buses, restaurants, shopping malls and any place where Israelis congregated in numbers. An army of suicide bombers marched into Armageddon.

The people of Israel retaliated in kind with brute force, ultimately isolating their Palestinian neighbors and denying any contact, other than military, between them.

The economic infrastructure of Jenin and the surrounding Palestinian Arab villages collapsed. Cut off from any viable source of income, many families stumbled into destitution. Young people were drawn to join the ranks of the militants by the promise of monetary rewards for their families. A cousin of Basam answered the call, was given a rifle, attacked a group of Israeli soldiers and was cut down without ever knowing how his sacrifice would benefit his family. It did not. Their home was bulldozed into oblivion the next day.

Basam had no work or income. His children were hungry and the only opportunity available to them was for Kamla and Salaam to venture into the Valley to find work among the farmers. An Arab woman and her daughter did not arouse the suspicion of the Israelis.

They made their way to Kfar (village) Shibli, a well-established Arab Bedouin community located just north east of Afula. Bedouin is a term for nomadic Arab tribes throughout the Middle East – many move from place to place while others, like the large Shibli clan, settled. Kamla and Salaam were allowed to work in the Shibli vegetable fields, were paid little and were given a meager wind-blown tent to sleep in. They did not complain.

Early one afternoon as they took refuge from the punishing sun and rested within their tent, a viper (a poisonous snake common to the Valley) suddenly struck three times into the right palm of young Salaam. Her screams and those of her mother attracted the attention of the local Bedouin who rushed to their aid. Salaam was in great pain and hysterical and the Bedouin said they must hurry her to the Emek hospital in Afula that was only minutes away.

"No," screamed Kamla. "Not to the Jews! Take us to Nazareth to our own people".

The drive up the mountain to the Arab hospital in Nazareth took nearly thirty minutes and the girl's condition was rapidly deteriorating. Upon arrival, they were shocked to learn that the hospital did not have the anti-serum that was needed to save Salaam's life. Her only chance was to get to the Emek Medical Center. An ambulance was summoned and during the frantic ride down the mountain, Kamla was frozen with fear as Salaam lay unconscious on the stretcher next to her.

As they raced the dying girl into the emergency room, Kamla could not comprehend the attention and care being offered to both her and her daughter by these strangers. Suddenly she was being spoken to in Arabic and told that Salaam needed an emergency operation. Everything happened so fast.

As the team of surgeons opened the girl's arm from her palm up to her shoulder in an attempt to drain the deadly poison from her young body, Kamla sat bewildered in the waiting hall. A nurse and a social worker told her that everything possible was being done to save her daughter. Her condition was critical.

Later, alone in the hall with images tormenting her of returning home to Jenin without Salaam, Kamla quietly wept.

The surgeon, an Israeli Arab, finally appeared, sat down and spoke with her in Arabic. He explained that Salaam was barely alive and being taken to the Intensive Care Unit. They did not know if she would survive.

"How can this be?" asked Kamla. "You are an Arab and you work here with the Jews. Why are you doing this for a stranger from Jenin?"

"You and your daughter are no different than any of the people you see around you. You needed our help and I hope we were not too late. May Allah be merciful."

Salaam spent the next four days on life support in the pediatric intensive care unit. When she awoke and her condition stabilized, she was transferred to the pediatric surgical department. It was there that I met them.

Accompanied by the department's head nurse who spoke Arabic, Hebrew, English and Russian, I was introduced to Kamla and a shy yet smiling Salaam. There were six other Arab and Jewish women in the room visiting their children. Everybody was nodding their approval during our conversation. Aliza, the head nurse who had seen more in her lifetime than most people could even imagine, joked as she interpreted – switching from Arabic to Hebrew to English so as to include everyone in the exchange.

"So what if you are from Jenin," she challenged with humor to Kamla. "You bleed just like the Jews. No?"

"How do you feel now among the Jews and Arabs of Israel?" I asked Kamla.

She looked from me to Aliza to the concerned faces around her and answered, "I would never have believed such a thing to be possible. May Allah bless you all."

"Will you tell your story to the people in Jenin?" I questioned.

Her immediate reaction was, "I don't want to go back there. I want to stay here." After a momentary pause her dark brown eyes opened wide and she seemed to straighten in her chair before quietly continuing, "Yes. I will tell my family and my friends. They need to know the truth."

Little Salaam – a young girl named Peace. Maybe her story together with so many others like it could be the threads of a fabric that might one day smother all the hatred in this land.

She Knew What Questions to Ask

"I know God will not give me anything I can't handle. I just wish that He didn't trust me so much."

Mother Teresa

"You gain strength, courage, and confidence by every experience in which you really stop to look fear in the face. You are able to say to yourself, "I have lived through this horror. I can take the next thing that comes along."

Eleanor Roosevelt

Kfar (village) Yona is primarily a farming community located near the center of the Jezreel Valley. Some of the most beautiful flowers sold on the roadsides during the weekends are grown there. It's a quiet, modest Israeli community like many others throughout the Valley, whose residents are mostly unaware of the historical powder keg within which they have chosen to live.

Avi and Rivka Naim's youngest daughter, Shoshi, finished her compulsory military service in the spring of 2003. Eighteen-year-old Israeli women serve for two years in the Israel Defense Forces (IDF). Many of them are able to avoid serving on religious, familial, health or emotional grounds. Shoshi, however, was eager to join but relieved when she was finally released.

She immediately began looking for a job so, like many young Israelis who have finished their army duty; she could save some money and travel outside the confines of Israel. Young people need to get away from here after serving in the military.

Finding a job was not so easy. Unemployment was at record levels throughout the country as the second *intifada* was taking its economic toll on both the Israelis and the Palestinian populations. The cafes and street corners of Kfar Yona became common ground for the young, post-military unemployed.

Shoshi refused to join their ranks and daily checked out any opportunity that was being offered. She answered an ad calling for security guards. Every restaurant, public building and shopping mall posted a guard at the entrance to observe, electronically scan and scrutinize each person entering the premises. A paradox of the *intifada* was that it destroyed many businesses while giving birth to a new security-oriented industry.

Shoshi was thrilled when she returned home after a twenty-minute bus ride from Afula and excitedly told her mother that she had been accepted after only the first interview. She would be stationed at the shopping mall. Rivka was not impressed or at all happy about her headstrong daughter's choice.

"You don't have to work as a guard, darling," her mother pleaded. "Your father and I are happy to help you until something safer comes along. Please, Shoshi ... we worried enough about you while you were in the army – especially after what happened to your sister."

"Oh, *Ema* (mother), don't worry so much. This is great – I'll be earning more than minimum wage. The people are nice and the conditions are good." Shoshi's mind was made up. She hugged her mother but could not relate to her fears.

Shoshi was trained how to observe the thousands of Jews and Arabs who would be passing before her, what to look for, how to check a handbag, backpack or tote bag and how to operate an electronic scanner. She also learned to be firm yet not offensive to anyone requiring additional questioning.

"Your job," her middle-aged instructor said to the small group of new 'recruits' as they sat comfortably in a classroom, "is to prevent a terrorist from entering the closed confines of the building where the effect of a bomb would be magnified several fold. With hundreds of shoppers walking around in a closed space, you can imagine the results. We've seen it enough times already in

Jerusalem, Tel Aviv and Netanya." He looked from face to face before continuing and then stared straight at her. "Shoshi, the reason we employ you and other young women is because sometimes an approaching female arouses suspicion. The odds of her being a terrorist are infinitesimal, yet it is our job to question and to search her if necessary while respecting her dignity."

Shoshi was given a new, crisp black and white security agency uniform, much smarter than her army clothing had been. She underwent a few days of on the job training and was then considered qualified. She took up her position at the entrance to the Afula shopping mall, located at the end of the Via Maris highway.

Shoshi returned home every day a proud young woman. She would pass other young people milling about the quiet streets of Kfar Yona and think to herself about the flight that would one day take her to exotic India or Thailand. She had made the right decision and she was on her way.

Her first week passed uneventfully but she was grateful that the shops were closed for the Sabbath (Saturday). Eight hours a day of vigilant attention while on her feet was difficult even for the twenty-one-year old.

Unlike others she worked with, Shoshi never had her mobile phone operating while on the job. She would not dare risk being unfocused if caught in a moment of crisis. The shoppers of Afula appreciated her presence.

That day in May 2003, Shoshi was partnered by Alex, a young Russian immigrant who carefully checked each shopper as they stood before him. Shoshi stood off to the side and studied the people as they came up the steps on their way to the entrance of the mall. It was a typically hot Jezreel Valley day (95° F) and she was glad that they stood in the afternoon shade of the east side of the building.

Her shift was to end at 16:00 hours but their supervisor came over and asked if she could stay on another hour or so. The girl who was to relieve her had some problem at home and called to say she would be late. Shoshi agreed without objection, as she knew her older sister had left the family car for her to drive home. She might even get in a bit of shopping.

At about 17:00 Shoshi looked at her watch and then caught the eye of a young Arab woman who was about to be checked. The woman was about her age, wearing jeans, a tee shirt and carrying a medium sized tote bag over her right shoulder. She was tense and unsmiling. Alex passed the scanner over her and it signaled that something metallic required further attention. As she was trained to do and without thinking twice about it, Shoshi quickly walked over and stood directly in front of the young woman, effectively blocking the open pathway into the mall. The next few seconds registered in her mind like disjointed imagery. Alex was saying something to the Arab woman in a silent charade. A man, second in line, stared blankly ahead. Out of the corner of her eye, Shoshi saw a woman hugging a friend, a teenage boy lighting a cigarette and a grandmother waiting at the curb. People were moving in every direction. The last thing she remembered was looking into the woman's sweating face. That was when the bomb exploded.

The deafening blast catapulted Shoshi into the air and slammed her into the shattering glass and steel of the crumbling entranceway. People and debris were forcefully flung in every direction, away from the epicenter of the blast that was the tote bag on the young Arab woman's shoulder. In a split second of fire, more than a hundred human beings lay sprawled, limbless, shattered, torn and bloodied in the afternoon shade.

Alex and two other bystanders died instantly along with their murderer. Amidst the smoke, blood, charred flesh and screaming came the first sirens of approaching emergency vehicles.

Within minutes, the most critically injured victims were rushed to the Emek Medical Center. The rest arrived in a long line of wailing ambulances shortly after.

Upon arrival of the first wounded woman, a call went out over the hospital's public address system that a mass casualty event had taken place and for all personnel to take up their assigned positions. All routine activity throughout the institution ceased. Surgeries not yet begun were cancelled until further notice, the forty people being treated in the ER were immediately transferred to alternate sites within the hospital, physicians and nurses from every department raced to the ER and operating rooms while technical and support staff took up their positions. The singular immediate focus of the entire medical center was to save as many lives as possible. Never had so many severely injured people descended upon the hospital so quickly as they did that day in May. Medical staff rushed from home to the hospital upon hearing the call.

Jerusalem and Tel Aviv have several fine hospitals and when a mass casualty event takes place there, the injured are evenly distributed among them. Emek Medical Center is the only trauma/emergency center in the Jezreel Valley. The lives of all the Afula victims depend upon the quick, highly organized and experienced care of the EMC team.

The trauma specialists in the hospital's ER were horrified to see the massive external and internal carnage the bomb had wreaked on the female lying unconscious before them. Nobody had any idea who she was, as there was nothing left of her clothing or anything identifiable to help them. A badly damaged ring was removed from one of her remaining fingers, labeled and given to a social worker. The woman was then rushed to the operating room.

Dr Kopelman, the head of Surgery "B", and his colleagues had just finished an exhausting day of surgeries when the call was heard at just before 18:00. As they prepared themselves for the inevitable, the woman was wheeled in. They studied what remained of her mangled leg and body. She suffered multiple internal organ trauma, burns, fractures and disfigurement.

"Where do we begin?" asked a young surgeon, not believing what he saw before him. "Should we just sacrifice her leg and concentrate on saving her life?"

Dr Kopelman sadly shook his head, took a deep breadth and said to his team, "Whoever this young woman is, I will tell you this, she is too young to go through life without her leg. We are going to save her life and that leg … now let's get to work." So began a marathon eleven-hour operation.

Meanwhile, the girl's parents, Rivka and Avi Naim, had heard on the radio of the bombing at the mall in Afula. Panic-stricken, they covered the 20-minute drive in half the time and were greeted at the scene with pandemonium and chaos. Rivka frantically dialed her daughter's mobile number, but Shoshi's phone was turned off. They left their car in the massive traffic jam and ran several hundred meters to the entrance where they knew Shoshi was stationed. They were screaming her name. Rivka cried out in her mind, "Shoshi … no, no, no …"

The first minutes after a bombing are precisely when it is utterly impossible for a normal citizen to obtain any exact information. Who was killed? How many injured? Was it a suicide attack?

When Rivka and Avi arrived, badly shaken and terrified, the bodies had already been moved away. There remained only smoke, bloodied moaning victims, bent steel, shattered glass, pulverized concrete and the shredded remains of the mall's tall red metal facade. Nobody could tell them if the female security guard was among the victims – dead or alive. Nobody would commit to giving exact information in those horrible moments.

They found their elder daughter's car parked where she had left it for her sister. They could not find Shoshi.

They raced to the hospital, refusing to believe what might be a crushing truth, and were met in the ER by a senior social worker who brought them into a quiet room off to the side. She told them that an unidentified woman was currently in surgery. She showed them the ring. Rivka held it in her trembling hands and tried to focus upon it. It was so badly damaged that they could not say if it belonged to their daughter. A neighbor of theirs who also rushed to the hospital accompanied the Naims upstairs to the operating room. Neither mother nor father could muster the strength to go inside. The neighbor went in and held his forehead as he shuddered, and identified Shoshi.

The young woman suddenly had a name and a family. Dr Kopelman went out into the corridor to speak with her parents. He began explaining the seriousness of the multiple injuries Shoshi had suffered. Rivka stared at the physician and asked, "Have any arteries been severed? Are the injuries to the internal organ life-threatening?"

Dr Kopelman went out into the hall to update the Naims several times throughout the long and complicated surgery. Rivka continued to ask, "What about skeletal damage? Can you save her leg? Is she breathing with the aid of a ventilator?"

After eleven tortuous hours, a depleted Dr Kopelman came out into the hall and this time removed his mask and sat down next to Rivka. He held her hand and said there was slim hope for Shoshi and that she would be spending critical time in the intensive care unit. He could not say if or when she might awaken. They should go home and get some rest. Miraculously, her brain did not seem to be damaged. Looking at the tired woman beside him, the surgeon asked her, "How did you know what questions to ask?"

Rivka sighed wearily. "How do I know? Do you remember the double bombing attack at the Beit Lid intersection in the mid 1990s – when twenty young people were killed?"

"Of course. They attacked a main IDF bus stop. All of the dead were soldiers on their way home."

Rivka gripped Dr Kopelman's hand even tighter before continuing. "Shoshi's older sister, Etti, was critically injured in *that* attack. You see, doctor ... I've been here before ... and now ... I'm here again." And she wept.

EPILOG

In March 2005, about two years after this event took place, I invited Shoshi to my office. I was going to the United States to tell the story of our hospital and my hosts asked if any victims of terror would be prepared to join me. Shoshi, without hesitation, agreed.

I was amazed to watch her walk, unaided, into my office. Her lovely face was lit by a warm smile and she radiated an inner peace. I was privileged to be in the presence of a true medical miracle.

We talked about her health and she told me that she was still undergoing hydrotherapy and that the pains were minimal.

She explained to me that she did not remember the blast. The last thing she recalled was walking towards the young Arab woman – yet she could not recollect her face.

I asked her if she was angry.

"At whom?" she responded sincerely. "Because I can't remember anything, it's as if this happened to somebody else." She rubbed her scarred hands.

"How do you feel when you enter a shopping mall today and you have to pass the security guard?"

"It doesn't bother me, but I did get angry once." She sat so calmly and then her eyes narrowed. "The guard didn't check my bag. I challenged him by asking what if I had been a terrorist. He just shrugged and waved me away. Instead of telling him who I was and what I had lived through, I went and found his boss and reported his inefficiency and careless behavior."

"So, what happened next?"

"I don't know … I went shopping."

The modesty of this young hero was as fresh as a gentle snow. I asked her what she planned to do with her life.

"I want to study physiotherapy. After experiencing the pain and then undergoing rehabilitation, I want to be able to help others."

Stuck In the Mud

"We make a living by what we get, we make a life by what we give."

Sir Winston Churchill

"Don't walk behind me, I may not lead. Don't walk in front of me, I may not follow. Just walk beside me and be my friend."

Albert Camus

I remember my son, Boaz, during his pre-school days. He was always a quiet boy who seemed to contemplate people in a manner far beyond his years. He maintained that characteristic throughout his youth, speaking little as he was seemingly preoccupied in thought. The most frustrating part was that Bo rarely shared his reflections and that made me feel left out, not a part of what was going on in his mind and heart. I suppose that as a boy I was not much different.

Today he is a soldier serving in the Israeli Navy and in the summer of 2005, Bo will return to life as a civilian. Military life is not a mild experience for any person, especially since they may be called upon at any time to place their lives on the line for the sake of their country.

My son has spoken more about himself this past year than I've ever before had the pleasure to hear. I understand very well, having served in the Israel Defense Forces myself for eighteen years, how the military environment is fertile ground for right wing and extremist views. I'm proud that Boaz has still managed to maintain an open mind and that he is more concerned with finishing his mandatory service than with killing somebody.

On his occasional days of leave, my son spends loving time when possible with his girlfriend, Karen, who is also a soldier. It is not difficult for a woman to avoid military service, but Karen chose to serve as an ambulance driver.

Both being residents of Afula, they enjoy their time off together wandering the nature trails of the Jezreel Valley. A few days ago, Bo shared with me an important experience they had.

Karen had her mother's Subaru sedan and in the late afternoon, they were driving over dirt trails in open farmland that was miles from the nearest community. It had rained earlier in the day and they suddenly found themselves sliding off the trail and into the mud of the adjoining plowed field. Karen unsuccessfully tried to compensate for the skid and ended up with all four wheels embedded up to the car's fenders. The sun was going down, the temperature was dropping and there was not a soul in sight. Boaz tried pushing the bumper but only lost his shoes in the thick mud. The only thing they could do was wait and hope that one of the local farmers would happen to come by.

An older model Fiat suddenly appeared and stopped when the driver saw the comical but sad situation. An Arab man, his son-in-law and the younger man's two eight-year-old sons got out of their car to see if they could help. *"Ahalan wah sahalan,"* they exclaimed. That's Arabic for greetings and blessings.

A combination of Arabic and Hebrew good wishes were exchanged before the elder man and the father of the boys slipped on their rubber boots and stepped into the dark mud.

The children brought rocks, pieces of wood and anything else they could find to try to push under the tires to provide traction. Nothing worked. The boys then found a large woven sack that once held a ton of sand. The elder Arab removed an axe from the trunk of his car and I asked Boaz, "When you saw the axe, were you at all worried for your and Karen's safety?"

"Not at all," answered my son. "I was simply glad that he had it because we needed to cut the large sack into strips to use as a towrope."

The two children played near the Fiat while the two Arabs and two Jews worked shoulder to shoulder, hopelessly trying to get the sunken vehicle to budge. They attached the makeshift towrope to both cars, but the Fiat was no more able to pull out the larger car than those people were of declaring peace in the Middle East. The air was filled with good intentions, but there was no hope of success.

"*Abba* (Hebrew for dad), those people were really something. They were covered in mud like Karen and me, their car was too small to make any difference, it was dark and cold, and it was clear that they had no hope of getting us out. It made me feel really good inside that they stayed with us."

After more than three hours of futile efforts, a four-wheel drive jeep came upon them. The driver knew those fields well and he told them to wait a little longer while he went to call for a tractor from the nearest farm.

Another hour went by and the Arabs continued to stand by their new Jewish friends. At one point, they all looked at each other covered in mud and broke into uncontrolled laughter. That might have been the sweetest music the Jezreel Valley had heard in many years.

The approaching headlights of the slow moving tractor in the pitch black of night looked to Boaz like something out of a Spielberg movie.

The farmer brought with him a heavy-duty rope, attached it to the car's frame and slowly extracted the Subaru from the field. When all were on solid ground, the farmer removed his rope, waved goodbye and disappeared in the dark. The only thing he asked of them was that they stayed on the paths and out of his fields.

The Arab family drove ahead and guided Bo and Karen out of the field. When they reached the main road to Afula, the Arabs turned left and their new friends turned right. That was the last Boaz ever saw of them.

"Who were they, Bo?" I asked. "Where do they live?"

"I don't know, abba. I never asked. They just drove off before we could thank them."

That night in the mud of the Valley had a profound affect upon my son the soldier. He learned an important lesson in humanity. He asked me, "Where has all the hate come from? Everything seemed so natural and right out there in the mud of that field. Why have we all made things so complicated?"

A very good question. Maybe, we are all just stuck in the mud.

FATMA AND SHARIF

"Unless you believe, you will not understand."

Saint Augustine

Jenin has been labeled the Palestinian capital of terror because the majority of the suicide bombers were bred there.

Fatma was born in the early 1970s in Jenin, a Palestinian Muslim Arab town of about 15,000 souls. She entered the world during a relatively quiet period in a very troubled region. Her hometown is located on the northern seam line of the West Bank – or, depending on your point of view, on the southern fringe of the Jezreel Valley (see figure 2 in the Introduction). Jenin is just southeast of ancient Megiddo. It neighbors the Israeli city of Afula whose 40,000 Jewish inhabitants enjoyed trade and open communications with the growing yet underdeveloped Palestinian urban entity through the late 1980s. That was when politics took precedence over humanity and the region was caught once again in the historical vortex of violence.

During Fatma's childhood, her father often traveled freely through the open fields that separate the two townships and brought supplies back to their home. In those days, it was normal for Fatma to enjoy fruits and foodstuffs from the fields and stores of her Jewish neighbors.

The Jews too would often travel into Jenin and save money through local commerce. The Arabs demanded less for themselves within their less-developed society so their prices for everything from automobile garage services to coffee and sweet cakes were much lower than in Afula or other Jewish cities. The interaction between the two populations was natural and relatively uncomplicated – a simple exchange of goods and services for money.

During "quiet times", there is a natural affinity between Israeli Jews and Arabs. It is common to see Jews greeting Arabs with, *"Ahalon, ahalon"*. This means in Arabic, "greetings", or *"ahalon wahsalahon"*, which is "greetings and blessings". It is as common as a, "hi, how do you do" anywhere across the United States or the English-speaking world.

Fatma was in her teens when the first uprising, or *intifada*, broke out in 1987. Her friends were often involved in throwing stones at Israeli soldiers or vehicles that would be passing by and she was shocked to hear of an Israeli citizen who had been stabbed in the Jenin marketplace. She had often heard during her upbringing of injustices against her people, but she could not place the jagged pieces of the historical puzzle into any kind of meaningful context.

As the violence and counter-violence escalated into general mistrust and hatred, Fatma focused on life and wed the man who would father her four children ... the first of whom was Sharif.

Basic medical care and first aid were provided by the Jenin Hospital and when patients required more advanced treatment, they were referred to the St. Vincent DePaul Arab hospital in Nazareth. This city, where Jesus spent much of his life, is located on a hill that forms the northern ridge of the Jezreel Valley and looks south across the plain of Megiddo towards Jenin. The city of Afula is halfway between Nazareth and Jenin (just to the east) and lines connecting the three population centers would form a triangle.

When Sharif was four he began complaining of stomach pains and six months later the physicians in Jenin realized that they were not equipped to treat the cancerous tumor they had discovered. They sent Fatma and her ailing son to the hospital in Nazareth.

The year was 2002 and relations between Israel and the Palestinian Authority, which was responsible for the Arabs of the West Bank, had degenerated into outright warfare. The blight of Palestinian suicide bombings and harsh Israeli retaliations brought death and suffering to the people on both sides of the demarcation line separating Jenin from Afula and the inhabitants of the Jezreel Valley.

Most of the suicide bombers originated from Jenin and surrounding Arab villages. A large Israeli military incursion into that heavily populated area has added to the long list of historic bloody battles fought in this troubled land.

It was in the shadow of this harsh reality that Fatma and her son Sharif set out across the Jezreel Valley for Nazareth, having been given permission to do so by the tense and suspicious Israeli military personnel operating the checkpoint at the strategic Megiddo intersection.

Any hope she had for her son's health soon dissolved into despair as the physicians at St. Vincent DePaul informed her that Sharif suffered from a grapefruit-sized tumor in his stomach that they too were not equipped to treat. They told her that the boy's situation was terminal and if there was any hope that it lay in Jewish Afula – in the Emek (Valley) Medical Center.

"No, I cannot take my son there," said the young mother, shaking her head sadly.

"Why not?" asked the puzzled physician.

"Because I am afraid. The Jews will take revenge on me and my son because of what has come out of Jenin. They are a vengeful people and we cannot trust them."

Her mind was set and she was trying to resign herself to her son's cruel fate.

The Christian Arab physician reassured Fatma. He knew the doctors in Afula and of their advanced capabilities in treating children with cancer. "Maybe something can be done. Sharif has no choice." What else could he say to her?

Fatma held Sharif to her as they both sat on a sofa in the doctor's office. The boy doubled over in pain and that was when she agreed to travel to Afula ... to step into the abyss.

A telephone call was made to the Emek Medical Center's Pediatric Oncology (cancer) department, a car was arranged for them and they were off on a 20-minute journey into the unknown.

As they drove down the winding mountain road from Nazareth, Fatma looked across the Jezreel Valley towards Jenin where her husband, her other three children and their families knew nothing of the decision she had made. Would they approve? Would they be angered? She knew of others in her town who were accused of collaborating with Israel and subsequently murdered by extremists among her own people. Fatma would somehow deal with them, but she could not face her dying child and do nothing ... even if it meant reaching out to the Jews.

The armed hospital guards, who checked every vehicle entering the Emek campus, had been notified and allowed their car to drive directly to the children's oncology building. Through her window, Fatma saw oak and palm trees standing tall in the well-manicured hospital landscape. Grass and flowerbeds garnished the paved pathways connecting each building and it all looked most welcoming. Their car stopped in front of a white one-storey building: the Pediatric Oncology Department … Sharif's last hope.

Fatma slowly walked through the entrance with Sharif clinging to her long traditional Muslim dress. She was surprised when she was greeted with outstretched hands and soft voices in Arabic, *"Ahalon wahsalahon,* welcome … welcome."￼ Dr Gavriel, a Jewish Oncologist and the head of the department also greeted her in Arabic and with a warm smile, he invited her and the boy into his modest office. An Arabic-speaking nurse offered Fatma and Sharif tea and cakes and only after they felt at ease did the session begin.

Dr Gavriel asked Fatma's permission to examine her son and it was much easier for her to agree than she would have ever imagined. The doctor's gentle hands stroked the boy's head to make him feel more relaxed and then slowly felt his stomach for what he knew was there. There was a lot of eye contact and understanding smiles between Fatma, Dr Gavriel, Sharif and the attending nurse during that initial examination. There also was calm and an instinctual awareness on Fatma's part that they were where they needed to be. In those few moments, her fears subsided and stereotyped images of vengeful Jews evaporated like a cold mist in a warming sun.

"The tumor is very large ... too great to remove surgically at this time." The physician looked directly at Fatma and spoke as his nurse translated. "We'd like to begin chemotherapy immediately to hopefully shrink the tumor and then later remove it. Sharif will need to be admitted today. These treatments will take weeks – and maybe even months. Do you have a place to stay?"

As Dr Gavriel's words sunk in, the reality of her awkward situation brought tears to Fatma's eyes. She was only a few miles down the road from her home and family, yet she was utterly alone with her struggling son. Her family would not be allowed to cross the checkpoint into Israel and she had nobody to turn to for support.

The staff of that cancer department had seen so very much pain and suffering over the years. They did not need to be told what had to be done for this woman. One of the hospital's Arab social workers spoke with a Muslim family in nearby Nazareth and arranged for Fatma to stay there whenever and for as long as she needed. The family would not even discuss compensation.

Fatma was not from a family of means and she had no way to pay for what would be the costly treatments her son would be receiving. Why were these people, the Jews and Arabs of Israel being so kind to her? They were supposed to be the enemy.

"First let's do what we are able to do for Sharif. We can discuss those other matters later," Dr Gavriel smiled as he continued. "Nobody will turn you away, Fatma. Everything that can be done will be done for your son. That is the way we do things here."

So began their six-month saga. It was after a few months that I heard about the mother and boy from Jenin in our midst and that was when I decided to speak with them. I will always remember that day in the early winter of 2003 when the punishing heat of summer was behind us.

I entered the Pediatric Oncology Ambulatory Clinic that is accentuated outside with colorful playground toys that hint of health and happiness. Inside I was introduced to Fatma and her son, Sharif. The boy was bald, thin and glued to his mother's floor-length embroidered dress. An Israeli Arab man was there with his child who was receiving chemotherapy and he volunteered to act as translator. We sat in a comfortable office and during the customary small talk, I observed the proud young Arab mother seated before me. We gazed intently into each other's eyes during an unspoken moment as we worked to construct an invisible bridge that might connect her world to mine.

We spoke of her home in Jenin, her husband and other children. "How long has Sharif been receiving treatment here now?" I asked.

"Five months." She looked to the department's nurse who stood in the doorway and they smiled at one another. That smile transcended borders and politics. It was the smile of mothers, and in it I saw hope for both Palestinians and Israelis.

Fatma told me that after months of chemotherapy, Sharif's tumor had been considerably reduced in size and then surgically removed. He was now continuing his chemotherapy as an outpatient.

The Jewish nurse in the doorway said she had to leave and Fatma rose to say goodbye. They hugged, and I felt the love that passed between them.

Knowing that other residents of Jenin have been treated in Emek Medical Center yet were afraid to speak openly of their experiences, I asked, "Do your family and friends in Jenin know about Sharif's treatment here?"

"Yes. And not only them. Because I am grateful for all that has been done for my son and me, I volunteered to tell our story to an Arabic language newspaper, *Al-Sinara*, which is published in Nazareth. My people need to hear the truth in their own language." She hugged little Sharif who, while connected to his intravenous drip, stood close to her.

I wondered if more Palestinians who were treated here would speak out publicly like Fatma – if that would make any difference. Could their voices turn back the tide of hatred? I wanted to believe that it would, but I suppose I will never know. They are not speaking.

Our translator then asked Sharif, "Do you know that Dr Gavriel is a Jew?"

Little Sharif shyly lowered his head and nodded yes.

"What do you think about him?" asked the man.

Sharif's voice was barely a whisper. "He's a good man."

I thanked Fatma, Sharif and our translator for sharing their story with me. We parted as friends and I wished them all health and long life.

A month or so after that, the day came for the mother and boy from Jenin to return home. There were teary farewells and long embraces where each was afraid to let go of the other. They were driven to the Megiddo checkpoint where Fatma's husband waited for them on the other side.

A few months later young Sharif's condition worsened. Fatma declined to journey again to Afula with her ailing child.

I do not know if we will ever understand why she decided not to come back.

Little Sharif has since passed away. He touched so many of our hearts and so many people who read Fatma's words know the truth.

Fatma has maintained contact with the friends she made in our hospital. Her story is another thread of hope for us all.

ABED

"I think of a hero as someone who understands the degree of responsibility that comes with his freedom."

Bob Dylan

"You must do the thing you think you cannot do."

Lee Iacocca

If you travel west from the Megiddo intersection along highway 65, you will enter Wadi Ara. *Wadi* is Arabic for valley and this is the main artery through the Arab-populated hills connecting central Israel to the northeast of the country. Half way through the *wadi* is the large Muslim Arab town of Adnon. The Israeli-Arab population is closely linked to their Palestinian brothers and sisters residing on the West Bank. The town's political makeup includes both fiercely pro-Palestinian and pro-Israel elements, and pragmatics, nationalists and extremists can be found on every street corner. When the *intifada* broke out in October 2000, the young men of Adnon rioted and blocked highway 65 and the Israeli police responded in force to this, and to other areas of Arab violence. Thirteen Israeli Arabs were killed that day, several of them from Adnon.

Historic animosities and lethal mistrust once again reared their ugly heads and cast a dark shadow over efforts of the people of Armageddon to coexist in peace. In the eyes of the Arabs, the Jews proved that Israel would kill them off if given the chance. In the eyes of the Jews, the Arabs of Adnon represented a fifth column who could not be trusted and would undermine the security of the state whenever possible. Four thousand years of history had taught these people nothing.

In 2002, Abed Dahlan was a seventeen-year-old resident of Adnon. He was born into one of the larger Arab clans, the Dahlan family, who enjoyed the respect of their neighbors. They are hard working people who pay their taxes and enjoy a lifestyle that would be envied by their Palestinian brethren. The Dahlan family were shaken by the violent events of October 2000, but managed to maintain an equilibrium that is so necessary to function normally in this part of the world.

One morning, as he had done countless times before, Abed walked down to the highway to catch a bus into Afula, only about fifteen minutes down the road. He came upon another young Arab he had never seen before who was already waiting at the bus stop. Abed noticed something strange about the large black backpack he had over his shoulder and when he saw wires sticking out of the flap, he froze.

Abed knew the bus was only minutes away and instead of returning safely to his home, he calmly walked up to the man and said, "Hi. Ok if I use your cell phone to call my mother? I think I might be late in getting home today."

Smiling, the man handed it over.

Abed thanked him and stepped off to the side. He didn't call his mother. Instead, he dialed 100 – the emergency number for the police. In an urgent yet controlled voice, he said, "There is a suicide bomber waiting to board the bus at Adnon. Please, stop the bus before it gets here and send help. I don't know what else to do. Please, hurry." And he hung up.

News like that travels quickly through the Israeli security network. The bus was halted a couple of miles away from Adnon, while Abed politely returned the phone. Even then, he decided to remain at the bus stop. He didn't want that man to succeed in his mission of wanton death. He also was not sure what he would do if the bus did suddenly arrive.

Within minutes, an Israeli border patrol jeep stopped several meters from the two lone Arabs who were waiting for the bus. The armed men got out of their vehicle and began walking towards the man holding the large black shoulder bag. Abed, who was slightly further away, smiled and nodded to the approaching men.

That was when the bomb detonated. The blast killed the bomber along with one of the security men and seriously injured Abed. He was rushed, unconscious, to the Emek Medical Center.

Following emergency surgery, Abed Dahlan was placed under armed guard and handcuffed to his bed in the surgical department. Everyone thought that he was an accomplice to the bomber.

The next day when he awoke, Israeli internal security people questioned him at length. They did not believe a single word of his story.

"Take your hands off me and let me see my son," shouted Abed's father at a soldier in the hallway who physically blocked him from reaching his son's room. "My son was on his way to Afula ... he has done nothing wrong! Get out of my way!"

More security men joined the confrontation and warned the elder Dahlan to leave, or be arrested.

Abed's older brother then jumped to his father's defense. "Don't you dare touch my father – or I'll ..."

"Or you'll what?" snapped a burly menacing soldier with a rifle over his shoulder as he moved towards the two Arabs who were then being restrained by four fellow security men. "Your brother didn't succeed in blowing up a bus. Is that what you are so upset about?"

"*Yah-Allah* (a common Arabic call to god) – are you all crazy? My little brother wouldn't hurt anybody!"

"Not now he won't. Get out – go home with your father and visit him later in prison. As for here and now – no visitors!"

The human wall was impenetrable and the father and son shook their heads and walked away. They were joined by Abed's traumatized mother and sister who watched in horror as the scene unfolded.

Abed's family was not allowed to approach him since they were looked upon as an Israeli-Arab family who had nurtured a terrorist.

Comments such as, "Shame on your family", and, "You don't deserve to live in a civilized country!" were hurled at the retreating Dahlans by other Jewish families who had come to visit their loved ones.

The Dahlan family suffered four intolerable days before the truth became known. The call that saved so many innocent lives at the gateway to the Valley was finally linked to the suicide bomber's phone. The handcuffs were removed and Abed was hailed as a hero. His family, bitter and disillusioned, was finally allowed to hug and kiss their son.

Flowers, speeches and a citation for bravery replaced the armed guard in Abed's room. A sour after taste of unfounded suspicion lingered in the atmosphere.

Abed healed and returned home to Adnon, but not to a hero's welcome. He and his family were greeted with mixed emotional responses; "Why did you get involved?" "The disgraceful behavior of the Jews only proves that you should have let more of them die." "That is the thanks you get for risking your life … being handcuffed like a criminal and denied seeing your family." "A Jew would never have been treated in such a despicable manner. Now you see the truth and how we are only second class citizens."

The conversations among the Israelis of Afula were of a different tone. They were relieved that the young Arab from Adnon was not a terrorist. That would have further soured relations between the two communities. They were sorry for the "minor inconveniences" to the Dahlan family, but certainly, they could understand the suspicion and necessity to maintain security. After all, it was the young Arabs from Adnon who had rioted and blocked the highway. Why shouldn't we have suspected him?

Abed is an exceptionally brave young man who stepped into an historical maze where generations of hate and mistrust meet at every turn. There are too few examples like him in the cursed Valley of Armageddon.

BETWEEN HEAVEN AND HELL

"Those who can make you believe absurdities can make you commit atrocities."

Voltaire

"Men never do evil so completely and cheerfully than when they do it from religious conviction."

Blaise Pascal

I received an anonymous call to my office phone in the hospital. An Arabic male voice greeted me, "Please excuse me, Mr Rich, for not introducing myself. I heard about the book you are writing and I think you should speak with my friend, Nabil. His story is most unusual."

I thanked him, knew not to ask many questions, wrote down the number and made the call. He was right about the story.

If you were to pass Nabil on the street, you would probably not look twice at him. He is just another average-looking, Middle-Eastern young man in his twenties who could easily be mistaken for either Arab or Israeli. Nabil is an Israeli Arab Muslim from a village not far from Nazareth.

"Our village has been around for much longer than Israel," he began, sitting back comfortably in the passenger seat of my car. He agreed to speak with me, but only in an isolated place where we could not be overheard. I parked in an olive grove overlooking the Valley, not entirely sure what to expect.

"That depends upon your historical perspective," I answered. "Israel has been around for thousands of years."

"I'm talking about the Israel of today. The fifty-year-old Israel that hates Arabs and takes our land." He shifted around to face me. "The Israel that kills its own supposed citizens."

"Are you referring to the events of October 2000?"

"Yes. My elder brother, Walid, was taking part in an "event", as you call it. The men of our village joined others from around here who were protesting Israel's occupation of the West Bank, Ariel Sharon's provocative entrance into our al-Aqsa mosque (Islam's third holiest site located in Jerusalem) when seven Palestinians were killed by his security people and other immoral acts against our people."

"The protest, as you refer to it, was a riot where a main highway was blocked, the cars of innocent people were stoned and the occupants were threatened."

"Do you have any idea of the pressures that were building up inside of us before this happened? While Israel took more land and more land, and trampled on the dignity of our Palestinian brothers and sisters, we were ignored. Who listened to us? We had no voice. We were threatened and our anger burst into the open – into your faces."

"Were you there?"

"Yes. A bunch of my friends and me were standing on a ridge watching from a distance. I was 17 at the time and Walid told me to stay away." Nabil's gaze was focused on the olive trees to our right. "We saw the police cars arrive. They were heavily outnumbered, after what seemed to be only a few minutes, shots echoed around us and we saw three people lying on the ground. Walid was one of them. I went crazy, ran down the hill towards him and helped carry him away."

Nabil was trying to control his breathing.

"Those Jewish bastards shot my brother in the chest, right into his heart. He lay dead in my arms and I could not comfort him. He had no weapon and had only been yelling - so maybe Allah (God) would hear his cry."

"It must have been awful. I'm so sorry, Nabil."

"The gates of hell had opened and I could only think of avenging my brother's death. I wanted the Jews to suffer for what they had done."

For a second, I wondered if he was about to take out his anger on me. "You're talking about something that happened almost five years ago. What are you saying?"

"I'm saying that I had wanted to kill Israelis and die doing it."

Oh my God. A suicide bomber sitting next to me and we're having a pleasant conversation in an olive grove. I was more fascinated than afraid when I realized that he obviously had not gone through with his plan. I had to hear more. "Who approached you?"

Nabil's icy stare returned to me. "Who or how or where is not important. They knew who to approach and when. I did not need to be brainwashed or indoctrinated to do what I wanted to do anyway. I just wanted the belt and the knowledge how to detonate it."

I raised my eyebrows in question and looked directly at him, hardly able to believe what I was hearing.

"At the time I only wanted revenge."

"You seem to have changed your mind." At least I hoped that he had. "What happened?"

"My father was a broken man. Walid was the first son and my father and him were very close. They even looked alike. I loved my brother so much. The pain in our home was too much for me. I wanted it to end."

"You must have been crazy with grief."

"I wasn't thinking clearly. I needed to move about on my own and try to understand why Allah let this happen to us. So, I went to Afula to mingle among the Jews."

"Your future victims?"

"Yes. However, it did not go as I thought it would. I was always looking at children with their parents and crying out in my mind – why should they be happy when my family is grieving? I tried to imagine what it would be like to be standing next to them when I exploded. Then I thought about our home and what would happen to my family if I went through with it. I then realized that I could not do it."

"Couldn't you have spoken to your father?"

"My father did all the talking and he would have beaten me if he knew what I was thinking. He kept saying that I was now the elder son and that our family depended upon me. He told us that the Israeli injustices would be dealt with by Allah and that our place was to honor the memory of Walid."

"So, how did you stop the wheel that you had put in motion?"

"I told the man that came to talk to me that I had changed my mind because one dead son was enough for our family. I never called them again and I stopped answering messages they left for me on my cell phone."

"They didn't threaten or harass you?"

"No."

"Almost five years have gone by since then, Nabil. Why are you telling me this story?"

"Why are you writing your book?"

I looked down into the Valley. "Because there are voices from here that need to be heard. It's not all hate ..."

"And it's not all love either," he interrupted.

"You're right. Nevertheless, the fact that you and I are speaking like this means something, does it not? Maybe the message here is that communication is the key."

Nabil countered with, "Maybe the message is that Israel must learn to respect the Arabs and to take their place among us and not *over* us."

"Among the Arabs, yes ... but not *under* you. Israel cannot afford to place itself at the mercy of Arab tolerance. Your track record is not so great. It seems to me that some confidence building measures are called for. Do you have any suggestions?"

He thought for a minute and smiled. "Well, I turned away from the belt and we are here talking. That's a start, isn't it?'

GREATER ISRAEL

"Treat the other man's faith gently; it is all he has to believe in. His mind was created for his own thoughts, not yours or mine."

Henry S. Haskins

"First they came for the Jews
and I did not speak out – because I was not a Jew.

Then they came for the communists
and I did not speak out – because I was not a communist.

Then they came for the trade unionists
and I did not speak out – because I was not a trade unionist.

Then they came for me – and there was no one left to speak out for me."

Martin Niemller

Afula, capital of the Valley, is a multi-cultural blend of Jews. The mixture includes those from Arab countries (Morocco, Tunisia, Syria, Egypt, Iraq, etc), Europe, the

United States, Ethiopia, Russia, South America, South Africa and every other place that Jews have settled throughout the millennia. The city has a religious traditional heritage but the influx of immigrants is slowly challenging old norms, such as strict Sabbath observance of the non-opening of places of entertainment and restaurants. In biblical times, the city was called Ophrahh and was the hometown of Gideon, king of ancient Israel.

Jacob is an observant sixty-six-year-old Jew from South Africa who settled in Afula. He wears a knitted yarmulke (skull cap), has lived in Israel since 1977 and closely adheres to the tenets of Jewish law. The bookshelves in his modest home contain the five books of Moses or the Hebrew *Torah*, the Mishna (six books of Torah discussions), the Gemara (volumes of discussions on the Mishna), writings of the biblical judges, prophets, kings and prayer books. His library is common to those found in other religious Jewish households.

Of Jacob's three children, his middle son's family has lived for the past three years in the West Bank settlement of Dolev. That is a thirty-year-old community of 150 Jewish families located just west of Ramallah, a heavily populated Arab center and the seat of the Palestinian Authority (PA).

Throwing his right hand into the air, he snapped, "Why do you use the term, "West Bank" when referring to where my son lives?" We settled into his living room as I contemplated his immediate reaction. "He and his family are living in Samaria which is an integral part of Israel."

"By whose definition?" I asked.

"If I may, my left-wing friend, I'd like to share with you some historical facts." He poured me a glass of red wine and continued. "Judea and Samaria, located west of the Jordan River, with Jerusalem approximately in the center, are historical parts of the Land of Israel. They are currently called the "West Bank", a name created by Jordan after the War of Independence in 1948 when Arab armies overran Judea and Samaria. Despite the fact that virtually the entire world rejected Jordan's annexation, and even after Israel drove the *occupiers* back across the river in the 1967 Six Day War, the phrase "West Bank" has stuck, and is used to the near total exclusion of any other." Jacob sipped his wine, shook his finger at me and continued, "The mountains of Judea are first named in the Book of Joshua, in the account of the conquering of Canaan by the Israelites during the creation of the Land of Israel. From that time to the present, more than 3,000 years, the name Judea has been consistently used to describe the territory from Jerusalem south along the Judean mountain ridgeline, extending east from the mountains down to the Dead Sea. The hill country north and west of Jerusalem has been known as Samaria since the days of King Jeroboam, first king of the breakaway ten northern tribes of Israel after the death of King Solomon. Judea and Samaria have been known by these names for unbroken centuries, and were registered as such on official documents and maps, by international institutions and in authoritative reference books right up to about 1950. When the correct names became a problem for Palestinian Arabs trying to make their newly minted claim on the land, it somehow became "politically correct" to use "West Bank" or "Occupied territories" instead of the historically accurate names Judea and Samaria. The whole thing disgusts me."

"OK, Jacob, I stand corrected. They live in Samaria. But doesn't current political reality take precedence over semantics?"

"Political realities can be changed," he snapped again.

"Yes, but at what cost? For the past fifty-seven years, the Arabs have been trying to wipe out the reality of Israel reborn and Israel has been trying to ignore the demographic Arab reality. Many people have died in the interim."

"That is pathetically true," raising his voice, "but we didn't initiate the attacks. We have every right to defend ourselves." He suddenly stood up and began pacing, becoming red in the face, "You yourself have fought in a couple of wars. Did you go against your will?"

"Not at the time, Jacob. However, I would prefer that my son and grandchildren did not have to fight, because it doesn't solve the problem."

Again, his right hand waved in the air dismissively, "God will solve "the problem" as you call it."

"Maybe. For now, let's get back to your family living in the West Bank ... sorry ... Samaria. If we somehow were to conclude a peace agreement with the Palestinians, do you agree that the Jews living in Judea and Samaria should return to Israel?"

"Absolutely not! You sound like some Peace-Now freak! *If* there is peace, then why should they not stay where they are? Arabs live in Israel so Jews should be able to live in Palestine – just as Jews live in the United States, Europe and any other country."

"What if the Palestinians didn't want them there because they say they're living on confiscated Arab land? Don't you think their lives could be in danger? When should Jews move, and when should they stay?"

Jacob adjusted his *yarmulke*, sat down and thought before answering. "As long as life is bearable, then Jews should live wherever they please. By bearable I mean that they are able to live openly and freely as Jews, with full civic freedom and without physical threats to their well being. If they don't have that, then they should move. For me personally, if the place I lived went too much against the laws of Halacha (Jewish Law) then I would move. But hey, let's talk about the land and ownership. Who says that the land in Judea and Samaria belongs to the Arabs? Successive Israeli governments since 1967 have called for Jews to settle in Greater Israel. We purchased some of the land legally and much of it was vacant and unsettled. We didn't steal it from anybody!" He glared at me as if I had committed some terrible wrong.

"Where do you draw the lines of Greater Israel? Biblically, it included the land of Jordan as well."

Jacob nodded and pursed his lips. "Well, we're not about to go that far." Then raising his voice, "God gave the land of Israel to the Jews and I see myself as a religious Zionist. We have a right to *all* of the land but for now, we must make do with what we have. God will decide what will be."

"What do you think about the disengagement from Gaza?"

"If it will help to control Arab terror and save lives, then I am for it. However, I have serious doubts that leaving Gaza will suddenly make them love and accept us."

"What about the wisdom, or lack of it, in having established Jewish settlements in the midst of heavily populated Arab areas? Gaza has proved to be an unfeasible enterprise. How about Judea and Samaria? Isn't that just more of the same?"

He was shaking his head "no" before I even completed my sentence. "Let's wait and see what happens after we leave Gaza. The fear is that they will fire on our cities in the south, unhindered by any Jewish presence. We'll know soon enough of their intentions."

"Jacob, occupation is the control of a foreign population by force of arms. Isn't that what we're doing in Judea and Samaria?"

"We wanted to live among them in peace. And for God's sake, it's our bloody land anyway! Their murderous terror brought about the occupation. When they decide to live with us in peace, then Jews living in Judea and Samaria will be no different than Jews living in London or Paris."

"Do you prefer the opinions of Rabbis or politicians?"

"Rabbis, most definitely." He said that with a defiant gaze.

"Why?"

His shook his finger at me again. "Because, for instance, my Rabbi rarely voices his own beliefs. His opinions are always based upon some proven, religious authority. A Rabbi studies for many years and has learned to analyze issues according to an ancient wisdom. I trust him as a more reliable source."

"Do you think the two-state solution is the answer?"

"Hah! It's a damned joke. The Palestinians have never shown any willingness or capability towards creating a viable state of their own. They have had their chances, but up until now, they've only shown themselves adept at killing and saying no."

I leaned forward and asked, "What if they disarm the terrorist networks, reign in the militants and move towards a political settlement with us?"

Jacob sat back, placed both hands upon his knees and shook his head back and forth, "Then we will have a real problem ... because *then* we will have to give up parts of Greater Israel. And it will all be because of you faint-hearted left wing secular types." He jumped up, walked over to his bookshelf and stood silently with his back to me.

The interview was obviously over. As I reached the front door to let myself out, I turned to him and said, "Shalom. Thank you for the wine."

CHOICES

"It is our choices that show what we truly are, far more than our abilities."

J. K. Rowling

"The strongest principle of growth lies in human choice."

George Eliot

"You've come to this point in time and you're at a fork in the road. One path leads to mediocrity, to a place where your medicine will never be known. The other path, the path of your heart, leads to profound medicine, to service humanity."

Anonymous

In 1964 when Shmuel Yurfest was nine years old, his family chose to move from Argentina to Israel. He learned Hebrew much more quickly than his parents and felt at home among his people. He grew to love sports but was even more drawn to books.

He had just been inducted into the Israel Defense Forces in 1973 when the *Yom Kippur* (Day of Atonement) war broke out. Syrian and Egyptian forces surprised and initially overwhelmed the Israelis on both the Suez Canal and Golan Heights fronts. Shmuel served in a combat unit as a medic and was thrust onto the front line of his new country's battle for survival. The trauma of those experiences forged his decision to study medicine.

Upon his release from active military duty three years later, Shmuel chose the familiarity of his mother tongue to study medicine in Brazil. He later returned to Israel with his M.D. and practiced general surgery for the next six years in the Emek Medical Center of Afula. Now he was serving in a medical institution that faced the Valley where, historically, more military conflicts had taken place than any other place on earth. The significance of this never entered his mind.

His keen intellect and special talents then drew Dr Yurfest to Southern Israel's Soroka Hospital to specialize in vascular surgery. In the year 1986, he chose to return to practice medicine in Afula and has been there ever since.

Over the years, his reputation as a gifted healer grew and the myriad of patients who were injured in automobile, home and industrial accidents owed the continued use of their limbs to his expertise.

In the year 2000, the character of the wounds he was called upon to treat changed dramatically. The Palestinian *intifada* brought with it a new generation of physical horrors and human suffering. The Valley of Armageddon cried out for more blood.

Bombs, bullets and shrapnel tore into the bodies of Jews and Arabs with a ferocity that even seasoned former military surgeons found difficult to confront. Week after week the anguish and suffering continued, numbing the senses of both the victims and their healers.

In 2002, hoping to stem the tide of suicide bombings, Israel sent a large military force into the Palestinian town of Jenin from where many of the bombers had originated. Israelis in the Jezreel Valley could see the smoke and hear the gunfire of the ensuing battle.

One fateful day a group of Israeli soldiers was lured into an alleyway where they were surprised by bombs that toppled walls upon them. Showers of bullets then killed those who were still alive. Thirteen young Israelis lost their lives in those well-documented minutes.

During the efforts to remove their dead comrades, Israeli soldiers found a wounded Palestinian militant among the rubble. He was transferred, under military guard, to the nearby Emek Medical Center where he had to undergo emergency surgery. The families of the sons, husbands and fathers who died that day are still asking themselves why that young Palestinian militant wasn't just killed on the spot instead of being offered the humanity he denied others.

Dr Yurfest was the surgeon on duty. He and others in the hospital heard of the battle in Jenin and were angered and disturbed at the carnage. From the window of the surgical department's family lounge, they could see the smoke rising from Jenin and the glass reverberated from those not so far off explosions. The Jewish and Arab physicians were each absorbing the news in their minds and hearts when the wounded Palestinian was wheeled into their operating room. There were no doubts as to the identity of their patient.

Dr Yurfest was immediately overcome with the stench emanating from his patient who obviously had gone many days without washing and had soiled himself in the heat of battle. The doctor's first thought was to open the window, but he could not risk the danger of infection. The appalling smell only added to the sick feeling he felt in his heart at being called upon to treat this enemy.

The main artery in the young man's upper right arm was torn and the surrounding tissue damage was significant. Dr Yurfest's mind reeled with the knowledge that this man may have been and probably was responsible for the deaths of his fellow citizens – yet he was now his patient. The choice to treat him or not was made on the battlefield. Somebody thought he was worth saving, maybe to gain vital intelligence information or to use as a bargaining chip in a future prisoner exchange. As an experienced former combat soldier, Yurfest knew that under different circumstances he would have killed the young man without thinking twice. That's the way it is in war; kill quickly and efficiently or be prepared to die. We are trained to protect our families, communities and people with extreme prejudice against anyone who would dare threaten to deny us life. The man lying before the surgeon had tried and failed. Now, Dr Yurfest was called upon to heal him. His feelings of anger and frustration only clouded his vision and confused the ethical choice he had to make.

His first instinct was just to amputate the man's arm. Nobody would have questioned his professional judgment. For a fleeting moment, the physician was filled with righteous indignation and could easily have removed the arm that had risen against his people and all that he loved. Clamp the exposed end of the artery and cut it off. Then another force took control of the surgeon's mind … an intricate bypass procedure could save the arm. Not the arm of an alleged killer, but the arm of a man. His years of training as a physician unceremoniously pushed his emotions aside. A large vein from the leg could be removed and sewn into the arm that would allow blood and life to flow into the limb. A decision had to be made. Abide by ethics or give in to a primal human urge? He focused on the body tissue and not the man.

Dr Yurfest ordered his team to prep the patient's leg. Over their surgical masks, the dark eyes of his Arab colleagues looked upon him with respect.

The operation took several hours, during which other senior surgeons looked on to follow the complicated procedure.

The first twenty-four hours following such surgery are critical in gauging its success. Every few hours, Dr Yurfest would step around the armed guard stationed in the room and check on his patient – but was unable to look into the Palestinian's eyes. After checking the wound, he found himself focusing on the man's hands. The uninjured one was handcuffed to the bed. They were so small and he wondered how such hands could kill. Had he given this man the renewed ability to kill again?

He found every visit to his patient more difficult than the previous one. On one such visit the young Palestinian asked, "So, everything is OK?"

Dr Yurfest thought about the significance of the "everything" and without looking at him, he quietly replied, "Yes".

When he was sure that his operation had succeeded, Dr Yurfest ceased to visit the man. He had done what he was trained to do.

EPILOG

A year and a half later, Dr Shmuel Yurfest, was seriously wounded in a suicide bombing at a shopping mall. He will never again perform surgery.

In his continuing role as a vascular surgery consultant, he was recently visited by a former Arab patient from Nazareth whose wrist he had operated on long before the Afula mall bombing. The Arab, not realizing with whom he was speaking, told Dr Yurfest of a Jewish surgeon who had operated on his wrist and that he now had no more pain. He also heard that the doctor was nearly killed in a suicide bombing. The Arab sadly said, "I hear he is not practicing medicine anymore. Such a pity … he had wonderful hands."

From Holocaust to Armageddon

"Generosity is giving more than you can, and pride is taking less than you need."

Kahlil Gibran

"Real integrity is doing the right thing, knowing that nobody's going to know whether you did it or not."

Oprah Winfrey

His father gave him everything in life he needed; the knowledge of how to differentiate between what people said and what they really meant, understanding of the laws of the jungle and the essence of humanity.

Dr Doron Kopelman, forty-eight-year-old Head of Surgery at the Emek Medical Center since the year 2000, sat back against his office couch as we began our discussion.

We looked at the beautifully framed picture of his late father as he told me more about him. "He shared with me stories of his fight for survival during the holocaust. Between the ages of eight and thirteen, my father was in the Vilna ghetto, the work camps of Estonia and suffered as a slave laborer building submarines for the Germans." He smiled as he gazed at the picture, seemingly lost in some childhood memory. "He told me how he together with his school teacher stole potato peelings from the German garbage bins and feasted on them to survive." Then he looked me straight in the eye and continued, "You asked me once, 'Who are you? How do you see yourself?' Well, I am a second-generation Holocaust survivor. Everything I heard and learned from my father I must pass on to my children. These lessons affect every relationship and determine my priorities in life. He did not tell me to become a physician. He gave me the power to make that choice."

Dr Kopelman was born in Haifa and has a sister five years younger than him. He and his wife have a fifteen-year-old daughter and two sons aged eleven and five. They live in the upscale coastal city of Caesarea. To get to work each day he must travel via the route of antiquity that snakes its way through the hills that separate the Valley of Armageddon from the Mediterranean Sea.

I settled back in my chair and asked him if he had Arab surgeons on his staff.

"Of course." His matter of fact tone was as if I had asked him if he drank water each day.

"How do you feel about working together with them?"

"I see no difference in that question than if you had asked me how it is working with someone who has brown hair or someone who is less than six feet tall. Perfectly natural." He leaned forward a bit and continued, "There are great Arab surgeons and lousy ones. The same as Jews."

I leaned back a bit, "Have you operated on terrorists?"

"Many. In the 1980s when the IDF was fighting in Lebanon, I operated on militants who were wounded and captured. During both the first and second *intifada*, I treated men who I know would have killed me if given the chance. An hour earlier, if I had met them on the street and saw what they were about to do – I would have shot and killed them on the spot – with no second thoughts. But here, in my operating room, they are my patients and I'll do anything I can to save their lives."

"Why? Was it your upbringing or the medical ethics you learned?"

He had to think a few seconds before answering. "I'm not exactly sure." He looked at the picture of his father before continuing; "There is not enough room in the operating room for politics. G-d forbid we should begin to make decisions based on value judgments of our patients … it would never end. Today a terrorist, tomorrow a thief or a rapist. It's the job of others in society to decide upon punishments – not ours."

His friend and colleague, a senior vascular surgeon named Shmuel Yurfest, was critically injured in a suicide bombing in 2003. The day that it happened, Dr Kopelman had gone home early because he promised his son that they would have an open-fire barbeque. They were wrapping potatoes in aluminum foil when his phone rang. A friend had heard on an emergency frequency that there was a bombing in Afula (where the hospital is located) and he should get back there in a hurry.

"During my drive back to the Valley, I called the hospital and told them to alert Dr Yurfest. Every mass casualty event required his vascular surgical expertise. That was when they told me to come straight to the Trauma Room ... and not to ask any questions. When I arrived, I saw my friend lying there near death. Dr Yurfest had suffered massive head wounds, burns and internal injuries. I accompanied him while we rushed to the CT scanning unit, speaking to him along the way."

"Will I be able to see again?" asked Dr Yurfest in near panic.

"Yes ... you'll be OK, I assured him – not knowing the answer myself."

"When positioning the moaning Dr Yurfest into the CT to determine the extent of the injury to his brain, I had to lie upon him to keep him from moving. My hands even showed up in the CT images of his head as my white surgical coat absorbed the blood that leaked from his body. As I held my friend firmly, I saw the face of the CT physician through the glass window that separated us. The look on that face told me everything that I did not want to know."

"After the imaging procedure was completed, Dr Yurfest asked me to anesthetize him." Dr Kopelman cried and held his face in his hands as he shared with me this story.

Dr Yurfest was transferred to the Neurological Center of the Rambam Hospital in Haifa, never again to return as a vascular surgeon.

Shortly after he was taken away, Dr Kopelman was summoned to his operating room. A few minutes later, Shoshi Naim was wheeled in.

"My first thought upon examining the critically injured young woman lying before me was to amputate her mutilated leg just below her hip. The immensely complicated and time-consuming procedure to save that leg would certainly endanger her life. Something deep inside told me to try. I decided to transplant a major vein from her other leg, but when I removed it I realized that it too was severely damaged and needed repair. Complication upon complication challenged me and everything I had ever learned. I wished that my friend, Dr Yurfest, were there to assist me instead of himself being rushed to another hospital, clinging precariously to life. You know," he said while gazing past me, "it was as if that time was some macabre fantasy involving somebody else and not me."

Even before the saga of Dr Yurfest and Shoshi Naim had forged their imprint upon the life of Dr Kopelman, other events had carved an epitaph into the legend of this man. The route of antiquity that led from the sea to the Valley had been waiting for him.

"In 2002, I was driving to work at about 7:00 on a sunny morning and traveling about 100 yards behind a commuter bus. A bright flash momentarily blinded me and I didn't understand how there could be lightning on a sunny, cloudless morning. The next second, I saw the bus in flames, realized what had happened and screeched to a halt. I jumped out of my car and froze in shock at the scene before my eyes. Dismembered body limbs, still twitching, were scattered all over the road, people were screaming and the carcass of the bus was engulfed in flames. I ran to the nearest opening and pulled an injured man out onto the road to do what I could to help him. I had no bandages or instruments of my trade to administer the life-saving assistance that was called for. Me, the great Dr Kopelman, a senior surgeon who knew all there was to know about the human body, felt helpless in the stench and vortex of the carnage. Other motorists rushed into the burning bus and pulled the dead and dying out. All they and I could do was drag the people and the bodies away from the inferno." He shook his head as his eyes filled with tears.

"When the ambulances arrived, I returned to my car and raced towards the hospital and the security of my operating room – fifteen minutes away. I called my wife and cried uncontrollably into the phone as I attempted to come to terms with the unimaginable."

A few weeks later while on his way to work and along the same road, after passing an intersection he felt a sudden jolt and thought that his tires had blown out. He stopped to examine the damage and then realized that on the corner he had just passed, a suicide bomber had prematurely blown himself up.

Several weeks after that and again on his way to work in the morning, Dr Kopelman found himself trapped in a massive traffic jam just west of the Megiddo intersection.

"From over the ridge ahead of me, I could see smoke billowing skywards – a sight that was burned into my memory from that previous experience. I maneuvered my jeep off the road and made my own path to the bombed out bus that I knew was there. This time I was equipped with a fully stocked medical bag that was a personal gift from Israel's Minister of Health. After helping the most critically injured, I jumped into an ambulance to accompany a seriously wounded bus passenger to the hospital. I just left my jeep behind."

I then asked Dr Kopelman if he thought there was any hope of peace between the Arabs and Jews.

"Everything is possible," he said. "Ten years ago did you ever imagine the disintegration of the mighty Soviet Union?" After a short pause, he continued, "By working so closely with Arabs and getting to know them as people, I understand that there can be peace. Things seem to get complicated on the political level – far from the people who are living the reality."

"Do you want your children to stay in Israel?"

Dr Kopelman looked at the photo of his father. "Everything that I have experienced and seen is nothing compared to what my father lived through. My family knows that there is no other place on this earth for Jews to live – even if it means fighting for our survival. I am a second-generation holocaust survivor, but my children are not the third. They are afraid … but they are home."

ZIAD

"Victory attained by violence is tantamount to a defeat, for it is momentary."

Mahatma Gandhi

"Nearly all men can stand adversity, but if you want to test a man's character, give him power."

Abraham Lincoln

The Christian Arab Manda family of Nazareth traces its roots back 300 years and have lived through the days of the Ottoman Empire, the British mandate and modern-day Israel.

In 1930, several members of the family decided to move southwards across the Jezreel Valley and seek their fortune in the hilly region of the Jenin enclave. There, in a modest, six-square-meter blacksmith shop, they began building hand ploughs for local farmers. Their business slowly grew into an agricultural manufacturing, maintenance and repair facility for all conventional farming needs.

Ziad Manda, born in Jenin in 1946, after learning the trade from his father and grandfather, applied his skills and acute business intelligence and molded the company into the largest manufacturer of agricultural equipment in the entire region. Today, it is a 10,000 square meter modern factory that any country would be proud of.

Ziad sat across from me, together with his thirty-one-year-old son, Bassam, in a small café located halfway between Jenin and Afula. Ziad was reputed to be one of the wealthiest men in the Palestinian territories and did not fit the stereotype I had in my mind of our Palestinian neighbors.

Our meeting began with a firm handshake and I felt the powerful hand of a man who had worked many years with steel as I looked into his dark eyes that had seen life and the world from an angle so different from mine. The hand of Bassam was softer and his face was less lined. He radiated a gentle, academic nature.

Ziad launched into a methodical historical monologue of the growth of his company. He shared with me the story of his trusted relationships with both the Jewish and Arab farmers of the region and how he introduced modern technology and manufacturing techniques into his business. He emphasized his uncompromising attention to quality control, from welding to design and I felt comfortable in the presence of this businessman. However, I wanted more from him.

I placed my now empty coffee cup onto the small table between us. "You are successful and obviously wealthy. I have no doubts that your fellow citizens are envious of your material accomplishments. How do you deal with that?"

"What people think is not my affair. I have a business to run and *that* is my concern."

"How have the carnage and the strife of the past few years affected your business?"

Ziad looked first to his son and then to me before answering. "The situation has not been good for business, but I am well established and have the staying power until things get better."

"And do you see things getting better now?" I was referring to the post-Arafat era now in its formative stages.

He settled back in his chair and folded his hands over his stomach. "I have been through many fluctuations in our tempestuous market and society. Up until 1967, Arabs and Jews roamed freely among each other's farms and cities. It was a healthy time – for the people and for business. The Israelis saw I was a manufacturing entity to be taken seriously and after my invitation to and participation in the Israel Agritech 1979 trade fair, my business reached new heights. Israeli kibbutzim and *moshavim* (cooperative agricultural communities) chose to buy from me because of the high quality of my equipment and lower than Israeli prices. In 1981, Israeli manufacturers took me to court in an attempt to expose faulty manufacturing techniques that made my low prices possible."

"You're smiling," I said.

"Yes, of course. That misguided legal fiasco resulted in their lawsuit being thrown out of court and my business received the official Israel stamp of approval – including your Standard's Institute endorsement. In simple terms, they were afraid of me, they were wrong and I was right."

"So, are you telling me that it was business-as-usual despite the first *intifada* (1987–1993)?"

"That was a time when Israelis began to grow wary of coming to Jenin because of occasional attacks against them. The result was a significant business slow down." Ziad shifted in his chair and leaned closer towards me. "The Oslo agreement of 1993 revived what was to be a short-lived period of hope."

"Short-lived …?"

"Yes. When Arafat returned from exile in Tunisia to the West Bank in 1994, our society began a downhill slide that we have yet to recover from." The controlled anger in his voice sharpened his tone. "The economy went to the dogs, governmental corruption raped our social order, militant gangs roamed our streets freely, public utilities fell into a miserable state of disrepair and the fabric of our society unraveled."

"And what did you, as a business leader and significant economic force, do?"

"I kept my head down and waited. I am not stupid. I saw the forces at work and I warned my sons against getting involved in any militant activities."

"You are known all over the West Bank and well respected. Why didn't you get involved in politics and try to bring about changes from within the system?"

He looked at me with raised eyebrows, like a father about to share an obvious truth with his growing child. "What do you think – that we enjoy democracy like you Israelis? We are decades from such enlightenment. To get involved in politics would draw unwanted, even lethal, attention to my family, my business and me. I don't need the attention nor do I want it."

"Are you telling me that people were/are not interested in your opinions?"

"Remember, my friend, I am a Christian. Our small community of 250 souls lives in a sea surrounded by about 50,000 Muslims. It is wise to maintain a low political profile. It is better to be invisible and alive."

"Were demands not made upon you to provide financial support for the *intifada*?"

"No. Arafat used the money he pilfered from our people to fuel the bloodshed instead of funneling it towards schools, hospitals and the economy. Also, money poured into Arafat's coffers from outside the country."

"What were you thinking during the height of the suicide bombings and Israeli reprisals?"

"I built ploughs. I knew the time would come when people would again work the land instead of soaking it with blood."

"Do you think that time has arrived, now that Arafat is history and a new Palestinian Authority is emerging?"

"It is too early to say. We must wait and see."

I ordered us another cup of coffee. "Today there is a border fence and Israeli military patrols across the land your family once walked unobstructed to get to Jenin. Does that bother you?"

"No, it is a welcome addition to our landscape. Before, Israel would take land here and there and nobody knew where it would end. Now there is a line dividing what is yours and what is ours. Now we know what we have and we can move ahead."

"What about the Law of Return?" I asked. "Do you think the displaced millions of Palestinians should be allowed to return to Israel and the future Palestinian state in the West Bank?

"Absolutely not … the idea is ludicrous and any sane Palestinian would be against it. There is no housing or economic infrastructure to support them; they would lack food and employment. They should be compensated and they need to move on. History is full of such people."

Looking at his son, Bassam, I asked, "What do you tell your children, Ziad, with regards to Israel?"

"I tell them that we need to learn from Israel how to develop our own society. Living alongside Israel will provide us with a good life. The two-state solution is best for both peoples. Live and let live."

"And what do you tell them about functioning within your own society?"

"I tell my children that they must be strong, even though they have a gentle heart. They must stand firm, in business and society, among their own people because the Arabs exploit weakness – even if it is perceived."

"Do you really believe that there can be peace between us – after all the mistakes on both sides?"

"Yes. Israel will leave the West Bank and forgo their occupation mentality. This is not far off. The greatest threat to the Palestinians is our own people. Not Israel."

HOPES AND FEARS

"I am a warrior. But only when it comes to truth. Freedom, as we have seen, can be co-opted to do many things. Some use it to justify their country's actions but that is not always acceptable, as one person's freedom must end where another's begins. So freedom by itself is not the path because if we follow only freedom, then we will keep coming to a standstill every time we 'bump' into someone else's freedoms"

Floyd Maxwell

We moved into his modest office, away from the moaning and hectic bustle of the emergency room. We closed the door and the sudden absence of sound caused me to momentarily feel guilty that I had taken him away from his work. With no time to waste, I began, "So, my friend, we have often skirted the topic of the ethnic struggle we are both a part of, but we haven't found the time for a serious talk. You are the Arab who saves Jews and I am the Jew who sees things going on around me that I'm trying to understand. We both function beyond hate and I need to know how you equate or justify or come to terms with the

Arab/Jewish conflict. Look me in the eye and tell me what you really feel."

He hesitated before answering, weighing his words carefully. "I understand your (the Jews) justified fears, but we (the Arabs) are not responsible for them. Two thousand years of living in the Diaspora among non-Jews who hated and persecuted you are responsible for the horrible fate you suffered that culminated in the Holocaust. Not the Arabs."

And so, we began our discussion. I needed to know what this man essentially thought and felt. This man who saved Jews, Christians and Arabs every working day of his life.

Dr Azziz Daroushe speaks six languages, is a physician with specialties in Internal Medicine, Cardiology, Emergency Medicine and holds a Master of Health Administration degree. He is the head of one of Israel's most active and renowned emergency/trauma facilities (Emek Medical Center/EMC), he is a Muslim, my colleague and my friend.

He was born in 1955 in the Valley of Armageddon, in the Arab village of Eksal where his family roots go back for more than 200 years. His hometown is located at the base of a hilly ridge that forms the northern edge of the Valley, just beneath Nazareth.

With the support of his family, he made major decisions early in life. After his college education, he traveled to Bulgaria where he studied languages for a year and then medicine for the next six years. Dr Daroushe returned to Israel and practiced medicine wherever he could find work, first in the south, then the center of the country and finally he came home to the Jezreel Valley.

"I needed to be here in this Valley. The hills, fields and olive trees are a part of who I am."

He married a woman from Nazareth and today has four sons. He has been heading the EMC Emergency Room (treating 130,000 patients per annum) for the past eleven years.

It's difficult for a westerner such as myself to read the dark eyes of an Arab. Facial expressions and body language would hopefully reveal to me, beyond his words, what I needed to know. "You've seen a lot of pain and suffering throughout your career and yet, I know that October of 2000 was an especially difficult time for you."

In October of 2000, the second Palestinian *intifada* erupted. It was a far more deadly uprising than the first that lasted from 1987–1993. With unexpected fury, the pent up frustrations of Israeli Arabs exploded in a show of violent solidarity with their brothers and sisters living on the West Bank, referred to by many as occupied Palestinian territory. Young Israeli Arabs rioted in their cities and blocked major highways, disrupting life for Israelis of every persuasion. The Israeli police responded with lethal force and in the first days, thirteen Arab citizens of Israel were shot dead.

Dr Daroushe moved in his chair as if attempting to find a comfortable position. "No, that was not an easy time. It was incomprehensible to me then, as it is today, how the Israeli police could open fire on their own citizens." He nodded as he continued, squeezing together the interlocked fingers of his hands that rested upon his desk, "I do not agree with nor condone the violent rioting and road blocking that took place. Young men were angry and, unfortunately, were not intelligent enough to find a more sane way to express their frustrations. Even so, that was no reason to open fire and kill so many. They were not shooting or bombing anyone ... they were irate and out of control. It was then that I accepted an unsavory reality ... that I, as an Arab, was a second-class citizen."

"Yet, you continued to treat the wounded and save the lives here of Jews and Arabs alike. Wounded soldiers and police were wheeled in. What did you do with your feelings?"

His palms opened and raised slightly to the sides, "I turned them off, I cut off. People who arrive in the ER need our help. This is not the place, nor do we have the time, for judgments. We do the best we can. Later, when I return home I have time to think. It is not always pleasant."

"Are you saying that you feel differently here in the hospital than you do outside?"

"When here, I am like a fish in water." Dr Daroushe's dark eyes narrowed as he smiled with sadness and continued, "Outside of the hospital I feel as if I am looked down upon because I am an Arab. Never mind what I do for a living or for whom I do it. I feel unwanted and suspected. Almost as if I'm interfering somehow."

I was reminded of an uncomfortable experience Dr Daroushe and I shared in 2003. We were both invited, as representatives of our hospital, to speak at an international convention of Jewish physicians who were meeting in Israel's southern port city of Eilat. Dr Daroushe, although a Muslim, was a renowned and sought after speaker and I, although not a physician, was invited to tell the story of the Emek Medical Center.

We met at a local airport in Tel Aviv where we were to fly via turbo-prop to Eilat, about an hour away. I arrived first, was whisked through the security checks and handed my boarding pass. I sat and waited for Dr Daroushe. He arrived, dressed as I in a business suit, and while standing in the ticket line was approached by a female security officer.

She proceeded to interrogate him in plain view and earshot of the other travelers with barbed questions and in a manner to which I was not subjected. He showed her his credentials and I intervened to vouch for us both being from the same hospital and that we were flying to the same meeting in Eilat. As she continued her humiliating questions, Dr Daroushe looked at me with growing impatience. Other travelers watched the scene with suspicion and moved away.

When the woman took his pre-paid ticket away for additional scrutiny and verification, Dr Daroushe began walking towards the door that led to the parking lot. "I don't need this, " he said with disgust. "Who do they think I am, a terrorist?"

I felt his pain and I was embarrassed – for him, a man who had saved so many of our people and for us - to have sunk so deep in the mire of mistrust. And he was still expected to speak before an international gathering of Jewish physicians.

"Azziz, don't leave now. Don't let these people's insensitivity ruin an opportunity that we've been given."

"Opportunity?" He continued towards the door. "After this humiliation, because I am Daroushe and not Schwartz, you expect me to go and speak to a bunch of Jewish physicians? I have my limits! You go and I'll see you back at the hospital tomorrow."

"No! We're going together. They want to hear what it's like to live and function as a physician on the front line of terror here in Israel. You are a greater man than most of the idiots around us and you need to rise above this shit and do what we were asked to do."

He stopped walking towards the door and sat down with me. "Besides," I said, "I don't like to travel alone."

We both spoke at the gathering in Eilat. We both returned home, each of us scarred in our own way.

I asked Dr Daroushe how he felt when treating a wounded terrorist who had killed both Jews and Arabs.

"I told you, I cut off and concentrate on the body before me. There really is no other way."

"What about peaceful co-existence? Do you think it is possible?"

"If you had asked me last year or before that, I would have told you no – there's too much insanity on both sides. Now, after Arafat and with talk of a more pragmatic approach – maybe two states for two peoples will work."

He did not sound convincing.

"You know what's fueling all this incessant hatred around us, Azziz? Fear – on both sides."

"*Al-nakba* is Arabic for catastrophe," he answered, seemingly changing the subject.

"I know. Israel's re-birth and independence was - is considered to be – the Arab *al-nakba*."

I sensed that he wanted to delve into this most sensitive subject as gently as possible. The door to his office was closed so I told him to go on.

Moving a little closer to his desktop, he continued, "What happened to the Jews in the Holocaust should never happen to any people. Nothing can ever justify such wanton slaughter. I can truly understand and sympathize with your people's fears and need for security." He gently tapped the knuckle of his index finger on the tabletop as he made his next point, "And I would have thought that people who had been through such suffering and persecution would be more sensitive to the suffering and displacement of others."

"The world accepted our right to return to Israel, Azziz. Why didn't the Arabs?"

"Because the Arabs saw the guilt-soaked Europeans as attempting to right a horrific wrong at the expense of the people of Palestine who had nothing to do with the Jewish tragedy. The solution to the Jewish *al-nakba* created the Arab *al-nakba*."

I listened, trying to find fault with that logic.

"Getting back to fear," he continued, "the Arabs feared a Jewish takeover of their lands, while the Jews feared being left defenseless and vulnerable. And, here we are. Insanely killing one another while our actions perpetuate the very reality that we fear."

"Are you afraid, Azziz?"

"I'm afraid of the rampant prejudice and racism all around me. I'm afraid of what that is doing to the fabric of your society as well as to mine. I'm also afraid of the Jewish and the Arab extremists."

"What about hope? Do you see any?"

He leaned back in his chair, straightened some papers on his desk and said, "Time may heal these very deep wounds. Like a body that has been injured and traumatized, it needs a long period of rest and quiet for it to regenerate and heal itself. The same applies to the Jews and the Arabs. We need a very long period of quiet and rebuilding ... coming from a place of equality. Denial and dominance will only prolong our mutual pain."

A Meeting of Minds and Hearts

"Beliefs are what divide people. Doubt unites them."

Peter Ustinov

They came from Nablus, Ramallah, Hebron, Jenin, East Jerusalem and Gaza ... the places many Israelis associate with Palestinian terror and *the enemy*. After decades of misunderstanding have brought out the worst in both Arabs and Jews, how easy it is to over generalize and stereotype an entire population. These visitors to the Emek Medical Center were directors of hospitals, medical administrators and healthcare workers from our Palestinian neighbors.

They were taking part in a course on healthcare management presented by a local Israeli college and sponsored by European countries. Two Palestinian groups have so far participated in this bridge-building course: one before the death of Yasser Arafat and the other after his passing. Each group spent a day in our medical center to hear and learn about our way of caring for people.

Lectures were in both English and Arabic, as many of our multi-ethnic medical staff speaks both languages.

The discussions were lively and our guests asked many questions and shared with us the difficulties they experience while administering health care within their society. They explained how a lack of funding, roadblocks, curfews, utility shut downs, physical barriers and general violence deeply frustrated them and often resulted in unnecessary suffering and a loss of life.

We were committed to keeping these seminars apolitical. References to the unsavory political reality encompassing us all were skirted by avoiding such terminology as bombings and by referring to the physical and mental injuries as trauma rather than terror related. Our efforts were rooted in respect for our visitors and an attempt to reach out beyond the conflict.

We discussed the health issues that affected us all as human beings.

Thirty per cent of the Palestinian groups were female and we were interested to discover how many women professionals there are within their society. Some of the women were dressed in traditional Muslim clothing including headscarves and some were dressed in a more western mode.

The first group we hosted, while Mr Arafat was still alive, openly spoke of their anger and frustration about the sad state of affairs within their society. When asked with whom they were angry, they responded that their political leadership was responsible for the lack of facilities and modern health care. They also said that they would not be able to say such things or speak openly about their experiences when they returned home. Fanatical and dangerous elements among their own people have killed those they viewed as collaborating with Israel.

The second group that visited with us, after Mr Arafat had died, spoke in different tones. They told of a new atmosphere of hope and of their aspirations for a normalization of relations between our two peoples. They spoke of their desire to be able to travel freely to come here again and for us to visit with them. They wanted us to meet their families and share in our common humanity.

The most unexpected feature when meeting with these people was to see how very much alike we are. Resembling Israelis, these Palestinian men and women are warm, intelligent, compassionate, feeling human beings with a wonderful sense of humor. Their passion is the quality that makes them even more like Israelis. No wonder that these two nations have caused each other so much pain by allowing their passions to reach such extremes.

The question not asked, yet perhaps answered, during those shared days in our hospital was, "Is there a way forward and a sane future for our two peoples?"

Another small step has been taken. We have proven

that it is ok to speak, to share knowledge, to dine, to laugh and to shake hands with one another.

Evidently, coexistence through medicine works. This laudable example should be focused upon and emulated. Who knows, from the living philosophy of this humanitarian institution, both peoples might learn a valuable lesson.

UNDER THE STRETCHER

"You've never lived until you've almost died; for those who fought for it, life has a flavor the protected will never know."

Anonymous from Viet Nam

"War does not determine who is right – only who is left."

Bertrand Russell

"War may sometimes be a necessary evil. But no matter how necessary, it is always an evil, never a good. We will not learn how to live together in peace by killing each other's children."

Jimmy Carter

"What difference does it make to the dead, the orphans and the homeless, whether the mad destruction is wrought under the name of totalitarianism or the holy name of liberty or democracy?"

Mahatma Gandhi

In 1973, I was living on a kibbutz – a communal farm settlement – in the Jordan Valley when Syria and Egypt attacked Israel. It was on Yom Kippur, the holiest day of the Jewish calendar, and my new home was ill prepared for the onslaught. All the young men on the kibbutz mobilized and went off to fight. Within minutes, they all seemed to be gone. I was among the few that remained and in the middle of the second night of the war, I was woken up and hustled away to help pull up the perimeter fence adjacent to the main road and dig bazooka positions. We were located on the southern end of the Sea of Galilee, several hundred meters below the menacing plateau of the Golan Heights, just to the east. Syrian armor had broken through the minimal Israeli forces and was a mere half hour away from us. We suddenly became the last line of defense and I had no idea how to operate a bazooka. The Syrians stopped to regroup and wait for logistic support to catch up. Fortunately, that lapse in their attack was the window of opportunity that the Israeli air force needed to pummel and drive them back.

It was 1975 when I volunteered to serve in the Israel Defense Forces (IDF). I was 28 years old, married with a pregnant wife, ten years older than the other Israeli conscripts and highly motivated to become a great soldier. Israel was in firm control of the West Bank, had soundly defeated the Syrians and Egyptians in '73 and was a power to be respected. I was about to take my place as a proud member of that force.

Basic training in the IDF was the anvil on which men were pounded into shape as the nuts and bolts of an uncompromising military machine. We were forced to adapt our bodies and minds to function automatically without sleep while under the harshest physical duress. It was as if the officers waited for us to cry out in utter fatigue and stress, "No more!" That was when they pushed us beyond the limits we even knew we possessed

Stretcher drills. The IDF equivalent to a mould where the raw materials are poured inside, they are all pressed together under intense pressure into a shape and the parts that don't fit are forced out and fall away. A stretcher drill is where one man (the "wounded") lies upon a canvas cot while four other men lift it by the handles onto their shoulders and carry him to "safety". Three or four other men follow closely behind to replace a comrade whose legs begin to fail him while everyone is outfitted in full combat gear that includes helmets, flak jackets, ammunition belts and automatic rifles. The drills began with walks of a few hundred meters to get us used to the load and within weeks they evolved into tortuous marches of tens of kilometers – up and down steep rocky hills. They taught us how to function as a team and to depend upon one another.

I went under the stretcher to carry a load that I would have preferred not to transport. I was part of a team who had a collective responsibility to our "wounded" comrade and to those who forced us onwards. We all cursed the pain that bore down into our shoulders, caused our back muscles to spasm and our knees to buckle. Nevertheless, I dared not drop the burden that I loathed.

We marched like that through West Bank Arab villages. I was so proud to be there under the stretcher. The homes were shuttered and closed with nobody in sight. I so wanted those Arabs to look upon me so they would see a strong tough Jew who was a force to be reckoned with. They never looked, or if they did, I couldn't see them.

My military training culminated in my becoming a tank commander in the artillery corps. One and a half months of active reserve duty, each year honed those lethal skills.

One sunny morning in 1978 as I was working in the banana plantation, a jeep drove up and somebody handed me a "tzav 8". That is an emergency call up order from the army that is only issued if war is about to break out. I was in shock as they hauled me into the jeep and raced me back to my home so I could gather my gear. I found my wife, kissed her goodbye and was off. Just like all those men who suddenly disappeared from the kibbutz in 1973.

While traveling to my base, I learned that Arab terrorists from Lebanon had infiltrated and commandeered a passenger bus. They were randomly shooting out of the windows at passing cars as the bus sped along the coastal highway towards Tel Aviv and certain disaster. A military blockade was set up to intercept them and in the ensuing shoot out, tens of Israelis on the bus, including a five-year old girl clutching a toothbrush in her hand were killed.

Because of that unprovoked assault, Israel invaded southern Lebanon to attack the terrorist infrastructure that was responsible.

Our battalion was among the first into the fray. Images of that five-year-old girl on the bus and other memories of Jews slaughtered in the holocaust seared my brain as I shouted out coordinates, aimed our canon and fired – again and again. The thundering cacophony of canon fire, smoke and the sweat of battle added to my rage and glee to be hitting back.

The years went by and I continued to do my annual reserve duty, even though the brilliance of my uniform began to fade. Meeting up with my old army friends was pleasant, but not as much fun as it used to be and the passion for the fight gave way to a creeping personal apathy.

1982 witnessed the culmination of the Palestine Liberation Organization (PLO) buildup and rape of southern Lebanon that borders Israel's northern Galilee region. Terrorist attacks across the border were answered by Israeli air force reprisals and the Arabs began attacking Jews in Europe. When Israel's Ambassador in London,

Shlomo Argov, was nearly assassinated by PLO gunmen, Israel had had enough.

The IDF mounted a massive invasion of southern Lebanon for which I received another "tzav 8". Goodbye again wife, bye-bye kids. Operation Peace for the Galilee had begun. Our battalion was again first in and we fought day and night as we advanced steadily along the eastern flank. My crew went seven days without sleep but we somehow continued to function and fight. All those years of training enabled us to act and react. After routing out who we thought were PLO terrorists, we discovered that we had been fighting the Syrian army who had slowly been creeping up towards Israel's northern border. We soon were sitting within artillery range (20 km) of Damascus. A ceasefire was called.

We settled in to our position and secured our immediate area. There were dead Syrian soldiers lying about and we had to move them, or what was left of them. One lay on his back with his green army cap over his face. I noticed the gold wedding band on his finger and I felt sorry for him and his widow. I wondered if he had children waiting for him at home, as I did.

There is no glory in war … only survival.

After about a month, we drove our tanks all night back into Israel. That dusty, noisy ride through the mountains of Lebanon numbed my senses. There were no cheering crowds to greet us or fanfare of any kind. We were not heroes … only a bunch of tired guys glad to be going home.

In 1992, after serving for seventeen years in the IDF, I received my honorable discharge. It was not a sad day for me when I returned my uniform and kitbag to the base where I had been inducted. I watched as the young inductees were being shouted at across the field and I never looked back when I passed through the gate.

Israel is not an easy country, socially, economically or politically. Life here is like being under the stretcher; having to carry a heavy load that we would rather not be burdened with and one that we dare not drop.

SUMMARY AND CONCLUSIONS

"There is nothing more difficult to plan, more doubtful of success, nor more dangerous to manage than the creation of a new order of things. Whenever his enemies have occasion to attack the innovator they do so with the passion of partisans, while the others defend him sluggishly so that the innovator and his party alike are vulnerable."

Niccolo Machiavelli

"I have a dream that one day … the sons of former slaves and the sons of former slave owners will be able to sit down together at the table of brotherhood."

Martin Luther King, Jr.

"The best way to destroy your enemy is to make him your friend."

Abraham Lincoln

I drive every day through the Valley of Armageddon, contemplating the series of historical events that have resulted in its somber reputation. This is a valley of contradictions; fertile yet damned, unremarkable in topography yet unmatched in its global implications. The easiest way to maneuver the emotional minefield of living here would be to walk around looking neither left nor right and staring straight ahead, accepting what is, ignoring what was and not thinking about what will be. Maybe not.

Are we simply trapped in a topographical oddity where major access routes converge? History confirms the significance of this fact. However, are we not the masters of our own destiny?

Just because John in Revelation said that the *final battle*, the ultimate confrontation between the forces of good and evil would erupt here in conflagration, does not make it necessarily so. Biblical prophecy seems to be pointing towards a significant turn of events. How we choose to interpret those events and act upon them are entirely within our grasp.

A bomb that causes indiscriminate death and destruction is infinitely more shocking and attention grabbing than a handshake or an embrace. I've seen both; Arabs and Jews killing one another as well as talking, working and dining together. The former represents a struggle to dominate or deny while the latter expresses a readiness to live and let live.

What determines the course of human history – power or hope? A combination of both merges and gives birth to reality or life, as we know it today.

In the mid-70s I was a soldier who went under the stretcher. I was an angry young man, enraged at the wanton killing and destruction that targeted my people, Israel. Therefore, I killed and destroyed some more. I aimed my guns and rage at those who aimed their guns and rage at me. Were my tank and bullets superior to theirs? Was I more righteous than they were? By no more than pure luck, I am still here while some of them are not.

Was I involved in some primitive communal act of survival or were my actions meant to solve a particular problem? A soldier's job, during battles against a designated enemy, is to fight. We give away to others the power to determine who those enemies are. As I look back, I see my seventeen years as an Israeli soldier were both a responsibility that I chose to undertake as well as an opportunity to grow. It's clear to me now why younger men, with better eyesight, more rage and an underdeveloped world view, are called upon to serve in the military.

My subsequent years as a civilian aimed me in a direction I never dreamed I would go. In 1997, while managing a large industrial factory, I suffered a near fatal heart attack. I was rushed to the only hospital in the Valley of Armageddon and when I awoke in the Cardiac Intensive Care Unit, I witnessed something that altered the direction of my life. Two physicians, one Arab and one Jew, were working to save my life.

Even though I had been living in Israel for twenty-five years, I still maintained an unfounded stereotyping of the people who made up this country. The vision of those two physicians standing over me opened an important door. When I walked through it, I found myself gazing at life in the Valley through different eyes.

In the weeks and months that followed, I discovered stories of humanity in the Emek Medical Center (EMC) that made me want to dig deeper. Jewish and Arab physicians were working together in every department; the patient base of this hospital reflected the 50/50 ratio of Jews to Arabs of this region.

The *intifada* that erupted in 2000 brought into sharp focus the divisions, frustrations, incriminations and raw emotions that engulfed both Arab and Jew. The curse of Armageddon was king; blood flowed like the waters of the Jordan River, cemeteries filled, while people of the Valley retreated into their homes and shuddered in horror.

The tidal wave of hate raged all around the island of the EMC, but could not break through its walls. Somehow, the humanity of the souls within survived; Daroushe, Kopelman, Abed, Shoshi, Fatma and Sharif, Yurfest, and Salaam, to name but a few.

While the cameras of the world's media focused on the carnage, I could not turn my eyes away from these people. In the midst of all the killing, Jews were treating

Palestinians, Arabs were saving Jews - and Christians worked shoulder to shoulder with them all. I sought them out, one by one, to hear their stories in an attempt to understand how their humanity went deeper than any shrapnel.

In so doing, I discovered hope.

With their help, I emerged from my kill-or-be-killed mentality and realized that the curse of Armageddon could just as easily be understood as the *opportunity* of Armageddon. I realized how easy it is to pull a trigger yet how infinitely more complex and rewarding it is to put out one's hand in understanding and friendship.

There is magic in communication and healing in the hands of human beings.

We now stand at the crossroad of human existence. We have the choice to reach out to one another or to push each other away. Armageddon is a warning, a challenge and an opportunity to choose. Shall we continue the fight to dominate the Via Maris or shall we share this crossroad for the good of us all?

Could it be that Armageddon is really the focal point for the forces of good and evil that exist within us all? The harm that we have caused to one another in this Valley over the past 4,000 years is a manifestation of the triumph of the malevolence that festers within our hearts. Maybe the final conflict that John referred to is that of our inner battle to overcome hate, prejudice and most of all ... fear of one another.

These voices from Armageddon echo the pain of the conflict and stand as testimony to a positive reality other than that which the world's media has chosen to focus upon. The quiet voice of humanity *can* be heard above the rumble of tanks and the concussion of bombs. It is essentially a matter of choice.

MY STORY

"This is my simple religion. There is no need for temples; no need for complicated philosophy. Our own brain, our own heart is our temple; the philosophy is kindness."

Dalai Lama

On New Year's Day of 1972, the American Dream was not my dream. At the age of twenty-five, I bought a large road-worthy motorcycle, left Detroit, the city where I was born and set out to see the world. I left behind my family, a promising career in the building industry and a Jewish, middle-class lifestyle. I had not the slightest idea where I was going. I only knew that I had to be alone and far from the security of family, friends and even my mother tongue. I wanted to find out what kind of a man I was; how tough and how smart. Something deep inside told me that the answers lay far from home.

I needed to be challenged, even threatened and was determined to break myself financially (surprising how easy that was to accomplish) – just to see how I would survive when I had only my head and two hands to fall back on.

While I was living and working in the Austrian Alps in October of that year, I learned of the horrific murder by terrorists of the Israeli Olympic team in Munich. The raw deal that I perceived Israel was getting forced me into action. I leapt on my motorcycle, drove through Alpine snowstorms and came "home" to Israel.

Twenty five thousand miles of traveling alone and some inner revelations prepared me for a drastic change in lifestyle. I began life in Israel in the ultimate commune, a kibbutz.

I married, raised three children and after fifteen years changed direction once again, opting to return with my wife and family to city life. We settled in Afula in 1988. For the next several years, I managed large industrial factories, worked under extreme pressure with little satisfaction and minimal remuneration.

A near-fatal heart attack in 1997 at the age of fifty recalled my father's death at the same age. He died of heart failure. That powerful catalyst forced me to re-examine my priorities and to change the direction in which I had been heading.

I understood that God had given me an unequivocal hint and opportunity to change the things that were wrong in the way I was living.

My special relationship with our Creator has guided me throughout my adult life. Although I was born, labeled and raised as a suburban Jew, I do not adhere to the dogma of any organized religion, and I feel no personal need for a prayer book or synagogue. I communicate with God at anytime and in every place. I have never felt as though I was not heard.

When my health returned, I formed an independent consultancy business and that was how I became involved with the Emek Medical Center. While hospitalized there, I had become aware of a story that needed telling. This book is one result of that new beginning.

A historic process is taking place in the Valley of Armageddon and you have the opportunity to become a part of it. The Emek Medical Center is facing monumental challenges to expand its facilities and maintain the technological edge in order to better serve the Jews, Muslims, Christians and Druse of Israel and neighboring Palestine. Join the growing international family of friends of EMC and take an active role in supporting Coexistence Through Medicine.

You, your families and friends are invited to visit the institution and see with your own eyes the reality of hope that this strategically located hospital represents.

Please contact the author for contribution details relative to your country and for visitation information. Thank you!

Larry Rich
Emek Medical Center
Afula 18101, Israel
Phone in New York: 646-546-5970
Phone in Israel: 972-4-649 4417
Mobile: 972-50-5737 641
Fax: 972-4-652 2642
Email: rich_l@clalit.org.il

You are invited to visit the EMC web site:
www.haemek.co.il